LONG EXPOSURE

LONG EXPOSURE

Stephanie Bolster

Palimpsest Press
1171 Eastlawn Ave.
Windsor, Ontario N8S 3J1
www.palimpsestpress.ca

Printed and bound in Canada
Cover design and book typography by Ellie Hastings
Cover photograph used with permission. © Robert Polidori 2005
Edited by Jim Johnstone

Palimpsest Press would like to thank the Canada Council for the Arts and the Ontario Arts Council for their support of our publishing program. We also acknowledge the assistance of the Government of Ontario through the Ontario Book Publishing Tax Credit.

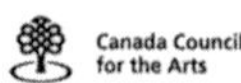

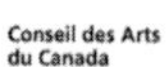

Canada

LIBRARY AND ARCHIVES CANADA CATALOGUING IN PUBLICATION

TITLE: Long exposure / Stephanie Bolster.
NAMES: Bolster, Stephanie, author.
IDENTIFIERS: Canadiana (print) 20250245329
Canadiana (ebook) 20250247879

ISBN 9781997508014 (SOFTCOVER)
ISBN 9781997508021 (EPUB)
SUBJECTS: LCGFT: Ekphrastic poetry. | LCGFT: Poetry.
CLASSIFICATION: LCC PS8553.O479 L66 2025 | DDC C811/.54—DC23

For the living and the dead

The snapshot is of a moment that will never occur again, and the long exposure is of a moment that never occurred to begin with.

—Robert Polidori, paraphrasing Dieter Appelt

All at once… something we could only have imagined was upon us – and we could still only imagine it.

—Philip Gourevitch

We're all living proof that nothing lasts.

—Son Volt

It is not something that begins.

Before there was land there was water.
A place silted itself up.
Around the time of the pyramids
parts of other places made this place.

Some of the youngest land in the world.
People came to stay.
The river was why.
Where some already traded on the high ground
a city of settlers suggested itself.
Later a café that would survive the storm
and in the swampy parts farther from the river
a place where those called free
and those who didn't get to be
went on Sundays to dance.

The bus moved through fields stiffened with heat.
Whatever happened here never.
Monuments pointing to a future rusted.

I was not in Ukraine I was not in the Zone.
Monuments once Soviet were now in Russia.
I was. Here was.

A city that *borrowed glamour from a hypothetical precariousness*
he said a city *inevitable, impossible* he said.

Where some used to dance some built houses
the city tore down to protests later made a park
some guides say's unsafe named for a man who sang
in a voice of gravel *We have all the time in the world.*

A bomb dropped on a ship
in a harbour off an island
far from the coast, the ship's name
the name of a dry and inland state
the colour of the Mars of the mind.

Displacement of a large volume
of water or
by water.

Long before I imagined
this street where I live I used to pass on the train
from Ottawa from Toronto to Montreal
thinking We're on the island now, we're nearly
in the city. Then suddenly water
at the end of the brief streets, a river wide enough
to call a lake. A lonely place
so far from where
I was going.

—When will we arrive?
—You're already here.

LONG EXPOSURE (New Orleans, Room, 2005—2006)

He didn't move the dress.
Polidori moved himself to make the dress
the centre of regret.

•

The world in the form of a storm
sent them out of the room.
Ran for their lives. With
their lives. Lost or left their lives
to fill with water and wind
or peel from the walls.

What they think of the room, if
they think of it, if they have lived
to think of it, doesn't look like
this. Ordinary
voices, TV, coffee.

2020—

It sent them out of the world into their rooms.
The world of their rooms.
The kids in their rooms.
The kids in the school of their rooms.
School of their phones in their rooms or their jobs.
School at their jobs in their ears for a year.
Or their fear.
The room or the lack of a room in their fear.

•

The passport, the jammed bags, the cab ride,

the check-in, the bag tag, the wait.

The gate, the seat, the take-off.

Ice or no ice. The napkin.

The *bing*, the buckle released, the icon for baggage.

The bag, more battered. The wait, the cab, the ride.

The name and the PIN.

The card in the door.

The room with a bed. The light and the sink.

The rest. The drive to the room.

The room no one's in but the one who's come

all this way to be in the room.

•

He went inside and with no power
he kept the shutter open long enough
for what light there was
to seal the scene.

•

Until he presses, nothing happens.
When he presses, the nothing affixes.
Prints are made.
Walk into rooms of walls, look
into the rooms on the walls.

•

The larger the negative, the more.
In the print of the wreck of a room
(smaller than the room, larger than
the mind) are things we wouldn't have seen
had we been there. (Some of us
were. Is there ever us?)

•

The opening: stemless
glasses, chatter.

This red, how did he get this red.
Or: This mould is baroque.

•

Not real art because he just looked.
Because someone asked for it. Because
a magazine. Because someone paid for it.
He didn't move anything. Didn't
make anything. Many
saw it. Because there was
an opening. Because he didn't
live there. It really happened.

•

It wasn't supposed to happen.
Keep happening.
The room breathing in breathing out.
—*It is happening again.*

14 May 2020

David Lynch does the weather each day.
Reports the after time will be much kinder, more spiritual.
Raises funds for free TM training for essential workers.
He makes small lamps.

•

Back on his own dime.
He opens the door of a house soft with water.
The smell of what it carried rampant.
A mirror seeped of its reflection.
Dead dog, a dead fridge.
He vomits again.
Opens the shutter and waits.
A kitchen scale wavers.
In the room he slept in, the mattress,
stripped, bares its old stains.

In the bar fridge, an orange,
drying. Set out beside the sink,
a razor, a canister of pent-up froth.
Next door another door.

•

As though rooms knew what would become of them,
as though they were skins or had skins or eyes or felt
anything, and a dog wandered through and howled and the walls
responded and I was the dog, the thing that trespassed.

•

Would the one who lived there
recognize it on a wall?

Before it was a scene?

Before it was a scene it was a self.

Called Café du Monde.

The dancing place called Place Congo,

Congo Plains, Place Publique, Circus Square.

Beauregard Square for a while.

Congo Square lasted.

I went in whitely couldn't find the gap
in the fence to get out the other side.

The fields didn't know
what they were. The monuments.

The factories, relics. We held our cameras
to the windows, the driver kept going.

Before leaving I photographed
the crooked carpet down a hall, a stain
on the wallpaper
I'd seen before.

Toppled by protestors
Removed by county
Removed by city
Removed by school
Removal authorized by unanimous vote
Removed by governor's order
Removed by Cherokee nation
Dismantled and placed in storage
182 and counting

A city hides in a courtyard,
in a pot on a balcony.

City where most
die where they came from, everyone
goes back.

Live oak roots buckle the sidewalks.
A major American city… depopulated
… a suddenness and thoroughness
war itself could not surpass.

Anyone sneezes, they have a parade.

February 2020

No one knew it was already in the hands that reached
from the float into the throng
(it was already in the throng),
in the coconuts they tossed, the coveted prize.

—Just kept thinking… This isn't how I die, this is not
the end of my life, and then… realizing, This is the way I die.

SHELTER OBJECT (Chernobyl, Fire, 1986)

April 2020

Someone set the fires
in the Exclusion Zone for fun.
300 fighters, 400, 100 engines.
How far apart are the men?
Some *tourist attractions* damaged,
the plant itself *unscathed.*
The worst air in the world
in Kiev but everyone inside.

The constellations made of fear. Chaos
where a shape was. Stars where a roof.

A fire where a place. The world
asleep in its bed. World irrevocable.

The heat unfathomable. They worked
shirtless. Already acute in hospital.

Soon coffins of zinc. Soon
they'd gut the wards of the dead.

Tried robots but robot death
seized their limbs if they were limbs.

So men scraped into a flat shovel
some graphite rods and dust. Tossed from the roof.

Count the seconds each man done
on to the next and the next of thousands.

Of hundreds of thousands. Liquidators past the limit
got more rubles. Their most important work.

Decades later after a stroke
one got enough rubles for 700 g of butter.

Too late they did not shout on May Day.
Fourteen days it took to die his tongue came out.

Leaves just opening. The parade stands
empty the children of officials already sent away.

Flash of paparazzi where radiation ate the film.
Years it took to die. His organs in his mouth she wiped out.

They'd wanted to be safe they'd wanted
the test done so they'd know.

If an enemy struck would the reactor survive.
Disaster as likely as lightning.

Men fished from a bridge. Loved a fire
all colours flashing old colours new colours.

Tourists come. The fishermen long gone.
The Bridge of Death they say. It's in a game online.

The leaves just coming out the forest
thinly green that first gold then red.

His mother asked when the bus was coming and in a while
she asked and again and then didn't and
he turned she was dead.
He covered her there in her wheelchair outside the Convention Centre.
Put a note on her. Came back
four days later she was still there.
The bus came for him. She was still there in her chair
bus was leaving he wanted to go to her National Guard said
You're just going to get on this bus. You must be on the bus.
The bus took him to another city.

A man fell.
Mud was sand or earth
until water made it made him
run through it and it was not still.

Worst drought in seven years.
On the map the rust the reds the darker reds.

Ask not where the Zone begins and ends ask
who gets to stay who has to go.

PACIFIC COAST (BC, Would You or Would You, 1942)

Would you or would you not flee when the day came to report to the address.
Skip curfew slip a note ask for people who knew people.
Coats with many pockets baby teeth in your shoes.

Torch your house so they couldn't sell your things.
Return to the country you came from.
Even if your unborn child was here.
They said you came from.
Feel like an enemy.
Become an enemy.
Sign up to serve your country.
Say nothing when the German POW was treated better than you and your
fellow troops.
Despair.
Sayこどものために.
Say しかたがない.
Let your husband go.
Let your husband build the road.
Choose the farms beyond the mountains to keep the family together.
Would you or would you not build the place that would house you.
What if you went to the front of the line.
What if you danced.
Some blocked the windows so elders couldn't see them dancing.
Two fell to their deaths in the river.
It's not as though it's over.
Are you lucky to have been born here.
If they did this to your neighbour what would you.
On the long walk to the station.
If you saw her go with her bags.
For the sake of the children.

25 May 2020

Darnella Frazier filmed it
Genevieve Hansen said check his pulse
Charles McMillian said *that's wrong man*
Alyssa thought she *was failing*
Donald Williams *called the police on the police*

No dove sent out no olive branch
no two-by-two, no
more later.

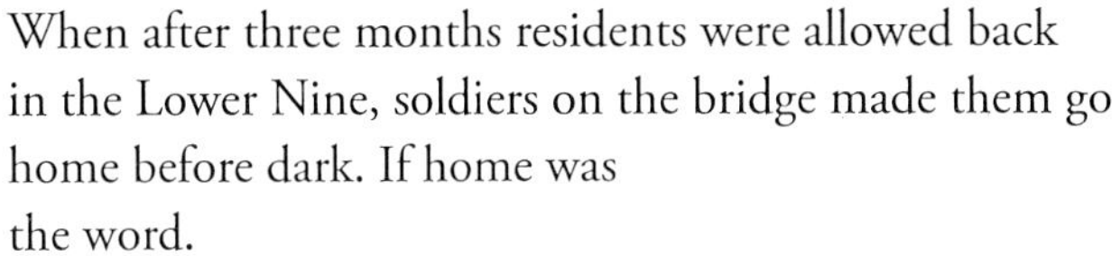

When after three months residents were allowed back
in the Lower Nine, soldiers on the bridge made them go
home before dark. If home was
the word.

First Responders not talking to the Army,
Army not talking back.

—Everyone went somewhere.

KATRINA (New Orleans, The Levees, 2005)

Some left days before
who had family to go to or cars
or who imagined making
a trip of it to an inland lake or
the Mall of America. Some held out
till the word "mandatory" till the whorl

Everyone went nowhere.
No one went anywhere.
Someone went somewhere and came home sick.
Someone went somewhere and came home fine.
Someone went somewhere and carried something
home unknowing into someone else's breath.

on the screen grew so loud they couldn't
sleep. Some sandbagged. Put boards
against windows unplugged each cord
lifted what they could onto beds onto shelves
filled trunks and roof racks. Some tried in those last
hours and their desire to be gone from what they loved
blocked routes out. Some sealed themselves in.
Made coffee and watched the screen as what
shook their houses came through live. They'd seen it all
before those palm fronds flung trash sailing past
and rain and rain and then no light no TV
no AC no phone no voice to narrate when
from his window up there in the station he saw
the water and looked again saw the water
spill over the gap looked again
and knew there was a gap and knew
it would keep coming knew the levees
failed and roofs not high enough to spare
lives from the failure of
imagination. If failure was not
faith the universe would never test
the levees. If not laziness not carelessness poor
training budgetary constraints not ego
arrogance lack of care. Some who left
came back. When they heard
how bad turned their cars around
returned with rations
space for someone
from a roof the Superdome.
They were turned away.
Whose imagination is stronger,
stay or go stay gone or come
back whose faith who loves
the world more.

Holding his wife's hand as long
as he could and letting go and watching
her wheelchair spin away.
He held a branch
12 more hours.

Body bloated by the curb the trucks keep driving past he keeps calling in.
Body at the booth in the Astrodome in Houston choosing Colorado New York Florida.
Body in a hotel room in Houston the vouchers running out money running out the
shelter closing down.
Famished body parched unwashed.
Body sweltering on a bus.
Dying on a bus.

Body in a truck in a lot full of trucks full of bodies.
Body in a body.

Some got born.

And where the overpass darkened my way I didn't go farther
the dark being dark the traffic fast my nerves
pricked how far is always the question
and what would I see but be.

Someone too close
unmasked or says a word.
(An old word, a mean.)
Who speaks up?

—And then the rest of your life begins… And really
your life is over.

LONG EXPOSURE (New Orleans, Address, 2005—)

The red dress a crescendo
a Southern Comfort poster, a cloud
of feathers on a wheelchair.

•

Someone hung a mirror.
Someone bought a shoe rack.
Someone didn't go to the French Quarter
unless visitors, or not often.
Someone suspended a trio of baskets from the ceiling.

•

Nearly half over 74.

After two days no dead counted
as Katrina victims.

•

Barking on roofs.
The hospitality of pineapple bedposts darkened.

In the rooms, frames
with nothing left. Or the intention of rooms:
planks held by nails and spaces, all our houses are.

•

This page ***may be too long to read and navigate comfortably.*** *Please consider splitting content into sub-articles, condensing it, or adding or removing subheadings.*

The union says
don't call it online call it
Emergency Remote Teaching.

Admin says
Lectures should be pre-recorded
digestible available asynchronous segments.
Chunking facilitates mastery.

•

Fled to a wind-whipped stadium,
a suit inside a shelter, higher ground where
the jobs are space just big enough to rest
a flame of ash a coffee can.

This was once someone's, a jacket,
a chairback, a plum
winced into.

•

Google Polidori.

Two matching frames,
a chandelier, the bulbs lifted like wicks.
A sandal, a car mat, the debris black.

The caption is an address.

•

Around the corner, someone might live.
Or might again.
A banishment, another place, kind
of time.

•

A girl home from school
slams the door, angry in a minor way
the future won't permit her.
No one notices the wallpaper,
the '70s flock thick as mildew,
foreshadowing. Only after
is this before.

•

Google Maps.
Enter the address.
Click the little orange man.
Drag me to the map.
Lift – it feels like lifting –
all in the wrist. Set him down

there. A field
and a bridge. The letter A in a red bulb
in the field. Then black.
Wait a bit. The image changes.

A sidewalk, a driveway in hot grass.
Where a house was, a patch barren of grass.
Shadow of a tree across the barren patch.
Some times of year there might be chicory.

A place of roses
some say it was
the buses took them from.

Called Lower Ninth
for down the river
closer to the sea. *That*
lower. In elevation higher
than much of the city.

Not Katrina but the levees. Since Betsy
it was clear they wouldn't do. Forty years
of not doing what had to be done.

To see how the other half.
To darken the other grass.

SHELTER OBJECT (Chernobyl, Hands, 1986—)

The poison climbed in and poured its soft sound out.
The face of a monster she wouldn't show a mirror.

Some looked into the explosion.
Some said it changed the colour of a man's eyes.

She cut her nails to the quick.
The sheets tore him where they touched.

Beloved unreachable
Staff in PPE as for the moon
Photos of themselves to point to: This is me

In labour at the graveside the baby
dead in hours. She hadn't told them.

Her beloved a reactor. Eye of the beholder.
The body shitting itself out 30 times a day.

Worse to suffer the shits or to watch.
Worse to tell the woman with the recorder.

Why are you coming here some said.
What do you want.

Radioactive meat in the expensive
salami fewer would buy.

Worse meat frozen in freight cars turned away
each stop. 600 tons. Four years the same meat.

Until they dug and buried where it came from.
Never as deep as the constellations are high.

The mind rusts or rots. What it held
falls through. Silence divided by silence.

To be sorted. To be remade. To be left
and leach into what earth. To last.

Her words before transcription or translation
were their words. Before they were words.

Still the cows spurted milk.
They shot the dogs.

No hat. Head back in the grass.
What you don't know won't. What you don't imagine.

How long it takes for safe is a mindfuck.
Plutonium 720 000 years.

They used to hold hands even asleep.
Lucky to live by the stained glass café by the pool.

> He said *I was close to something then.*
> *I haven't had that feeling again even in love.*

I will read it again how she cleaned
his mouth with her hand I will wash my hands.

British Columbia Security Commission Report:
October 31, 1942

Road camp projects	*986*
Sugar Beets, Alberta	*2,585*
Manitoba	*1,053*
Ontario (males)	*350*
Slocan Valley	*4,764*

30 April 2020

Vancouver's Chinese Cultural Centre
targeted. There's a timeline of recent
anti-Asian incidents, a website
someone updates.

(Slocan City, Bay Farm, Popoff, Lemon Creek)

Tashme	*2,624*
New Denver/Roseberry	*1,701*
Greenwood	*1,203*
Kaslo	*965*
Sandon	*920*
Self-Supporting Projects	*1,164*
Independent Projects	*431*
Special Permits	*1,337*
Repatriated to Japan	*42*
Evacuated voluntarily	*579*
Internment camps	*699*
In detention, Vancouver	*57*
Hastings Park, Hospital	*105*
TOTAL	*21,079*

There were 94 who were partners
in mixed marriages, with 100
off-spring, who were allowed
to remain on the coast.

The thousands at the border the children
the parents the distance.
The expectation the reality.

None of the thousands waiting
at Louis Armstrong airport thought:
I'm part of the New Orleans diaspora.

Oh I'm dyin' again! said Bugs
when he learned the penguin he'd helped
from Brooklyn to the South Pole
was from Hoboken. Its tears
froze to cubes. Bugs shoved the bird
into the hands of a stubble-faced
fellow American down on his luck
and fled. Laughing hysterically
the weight of the world.

HASTINGS PARK (BC, Exhibition Grounds, 1942)

By boat by train by bus citizens came or parked
by the Chute the Chute handed over the keys.

Women in the cattle barns men where used to be horses
and stands from which to watch.

The stink the twitches in the straw
stuffed into sheets to make mattresses.

They starved or sickened and shat.
No food if you arrived at night.

The food was slop. Sheets hung
to turn the stalls to rooms. They were not.

Meanwhile those fleeing homes
turned unsafe drown in the sea
whose colour this season's paint was named for.

Nestlé wants to bottle the desert.
Of course I enter my address.
Erica the world's northernmost elephant all alone in Edmonton.
Click.

Woman burned by her brother.
Two hundred and fifty million tons of plastic.
Reunite prisoner with her children.
Sell ugly fruit.
Help them stay in Canada.
Will you join the March of the Mothers of the Disappeared in Mexico?

Some did not survive.
Sometimes the less said.
The mind supplies.

Sometimes to look
is merciful, sometimes
to turn away.

WAVE (Tōhoku, Watch, 2011—)

A few moments to behold the end
before it came.
A force of anger but without anger.
Leaving a field of what
were belongings.

Nothing, then the sound
of nothing. As the water swirls the van,
nudges the house from its ground, only a tear and a squeal.
A family on a roof, a purse in a hand,
water takes. Get bigger,
make room. The sound
a sponge filling.

Some roofs weren't high enough.
Her phone found, friends send birthday greetings.

On YouTube the wave carries
dolls and doghouses it carries hangers
with the clothes still on them people with the clothes
still. Watch
full screen.

Her mother feeds her favourite meals to the sea.
What she thinks is a flower set before her.

Did the teachers see past the ones whose cheeks they'd wiped
whose hands they'd held to make the characters correctly did they
see a thing alive so wrong one couldn't call it water
but yes and closer and outran thought.

I want to watch but not the bodies
the retching crews want when he
went in with his camera
when it was safe to be shown.
Click "donate."

The first thing the last was a force that could not be
moved that moved and lifted
with the strength of myth the sky grey as usual
and under and a dog and under and a need.
Thought of the first arms. A cry
filled with water or just water end
of the world beginning.

I used to worry in the dark about
them dying, my parents. Watching *Barney Miller*
in the other room or *Taxi*, sad
music that meant late. It wasn't
that late.

Waiting for your FEMA trailer
while it sat in a lot. Then waiting
for electrical. Then the thin mattress
if you could call it the flimsy
table in a storm the whole thing shook
you loose.

LONG EXPOSURE (New Orleans, Address, *bis*, after 2005)

A year passes or more and next time
next door's a house with a fence. A fresh
driveway. Beside it, the pavement
still cracked. Numerals that were
the address sprayed across the cracks.
An A in a bulb in the field.
Floating there above the lawn.
Lawn's back!
The A casts a shadow.

The map of the spread of the red.
The seep off the charts the mould in the walls
the same places enduring the same
wasting away the story the same
in different voices different versions never
the same.

•

Next door, iron screens across
and on the pole out front a bent sign,
DRUG FREE. Zone's the missing
word. A bin left out.

Once a week a truck picks up the junk
and keeps on down the road.

Not far off, a tall wall. Behind it
the river.

•

When I pull out and out
the A is still there, the bulb
as large as New Orleans.

•

It must be quiet, nights, with all that space around.

Many said *Mother nature at her worst*
The Mother of All Storms.

Arlene Brett Cindy Dennis Emily Franklin Gert Harvey Irene (Tropical

Depression Ten) Jose Katrina Lee Maria Nate Ophelia Philippe Rita

(Tropical Depression Nineteen) Stan (Unnamed Subtropical Storm) Tammy

(Subtropical Depression Twenty-two) Vince Wilma Alpha Beta Gamma

Delta Epsilon Zeta

Retired the most deadly. The rest returned in 2011,
2017, 2023.

"Unprecedented"
but 1918.
AIDS.
Zika.
Ebola.
SARS.
MERS.

Katrina's popularity dropped
over 100 spots and kept
dropping. In Louisiana,
babies named Katrina jumped
from eight the year before the storm to 15;
in Mississippi, from seven to 24.

Karen down 171 spots to 831,
fallen from 660 in 2019.

When she leaves, the room bleeds.
Clots slick and big as eggs.
Bigger and you call for help.
It hurts when it retracts.
A vestibule, a closet.
A drawer until a little drawstring bag
not even a lipstick not even a mirror.

SHELTER OBJECT (Chernobyl, Matryoshka, 1986—)

A woman and a boy awake.
The window open. A wife a son.

Alone at home alone.
A corridor of fire. If those colours were.

The rods leaping in their sheaths.
Leaping as though joy as though anger.

As though meaning. No birds.
Some knew then the world wrong.

That night the sky of stars unchanged.
Everyone under them. I was falling in love.

The work of men. The women are carers.
I was watching the news I was crimping my hair.

Soon they changed acceptable
radiation levels. Soon everyone was safe.

Children of thyroid of the hospital.
Some eat and are not eaten some pass it on.

The dolls smaller and smaller the faces.
The fields still trembling green.

A liquidator's daughter's heart born wrong
a granddaughter's. The curtains the sinks the milk.

The water underground The Dnieper.
How do you pronounce. What do they know.

I say knowing next to nothing.
A quiet place bordering a void.

May 2020

Soon they needed teachers over 60.
No more exemptions.
Soon everyone was safe.

The harp seal or the manatee.

Pink or lilac.

SFU or UBC.

Basement or first floor.

This one or the second.

Tenure-track or freelance.

Transfer at JFK or Atlanta.

Hotel or Airbnb.

Business or pleasure.

He does not wear the coat so much
as inhabit it, always looking
slightly askance like an old woman
peeking out from behind
the curtain, even when out on the street.
He is content to observe
life, always slightly bored and often
waiting, if only
for a bus. Failing that he will watch
other people waiting for a bus. He has the patience
of a tree, or a bench
in its shade.

Had this been Cambodia.
Nicaragua.
Had I fallen in a waste place.
Thinned to ribs.
Turned away.
My words lodged behind my eyes.
The choice made by silence by stasis.
With my last force who would I put first.
Mother father brother
husband daughter daughter
me.

LONG EXPOSURE (New Orleans, Mirror, 2005—)

2520 Deslondes Street.
Spelled wrong.

A house and a space.
    Add a missing place.

Fence and fields and fields and paved
patches like shadow.

https://www.google.ca/maps/@29.9773572,-90.0193414,3a,75y,
190.92h,104.84t/data=!3m7!1e1!3m5!1s74i49g9VTfxA_oPAN
1PioA!2e0!6shttps:%2F%2Fstreetviewpixels-pa.googleapis.
com%2Fv1%2Fthumbnail%3Fcb_client%3Dmaps_sv.tactile%26
w%3D900%26h%3D600%26pitch%3D-14.84364791962011%
26panoid%3D74i49g9VTfxA_oPAN1PioA%26yaw%3D190.9235
951753525!7i3328!8i1664?hl=en&entry=ttu&g_ep=EgoyMDI1M
DUxMS4wIKXMDSoASAFQAw%3D%3D

When people could they climbed when they could open
the roof with their axes if they had axes with their hands
if they could when they could breathe they breathed
when they could swim. When people couldn't
held trees they held roofs when they couldn't let go.

•

People liked where they lived they had chandeliers
they had pictures with elaborate frames had
growth on the walls in the shapes of enlarged microbes

or the mask of pregnancy or maps
of made-up places.

•

Came home each day, weary,
hungry, the tree giving
just shade for a beer.

The babies older each day.
Who won't be raised here?

•

The eloquence goes unmeasured.
Eloquence the banister dust.

A mirror reveals its back of metal.

After dark, the back windows of the house out back
project themselves. Backlit like Wall's lightboxes.

April 2020

Glitchy wifi kicked me out.
Came back to a screen of empty rooms.
I mean frames of views onto rooms.
Into rooms.
I mean the class had gone on break.
I'd seen this before.
Someone said Hey you have to write a book
called Rooms with No One in Them,
I said I've been writing it for over ten years.

Image search for Polidori:

Three ruined rooms, New Orleans

One parlour of decaying grandeur, Havana

John William Polidori, author of *The Vampyre*

A wall at Versailles, with portraits, richly papered

View from citadel, Amman, Jordan, roofs and roofs and little windows

Polidori sausage

What does he look like again?

Badpanda22 says *Beautiful destruction… truly captivating*

Vasare says *omg love these photographs*!

There he is in his vest

Chernobyl auditorium, empty

There's a home improved by a driveway where the workers installed
a circle of unistone as a surprise windows all redone
year by year as savings grew a new front door that cost more
than a ten-day vacation a year's supply of food
for a family of six somewhere a solarium an office
where a garage was a shed where lawn was ferns and rhododendrons
false spirea a.k.a. astilbe sand cherry true spirea gentians varieties
of lilies lupin phlox goldenrod hydrangea wild
and cultivated columbine ferns and ferns and
hostas azalea ornamental grasses mock orange rudbeckia
oh yes and a deck and where the catalpa was
a spreading mass of St. John's wort and where
a crabapple was a honey locust and where a crabapple

was an American linden and where guests sometimes stayed
a girl of nearly eleven and where a desk a girl of nearly seven and where
a couple watched films and laughed two bicker
over how to load the dishwasher and who
gets to not eat her meat

TASHME (BC, TA-SH-ME, 1942—)

Taylor Shirras Mead –
the men who made it named it
for their names.
Those letters worn on the chests of majorettes,
stitched into handkerchiefs
in classes in a barn to send to friends
in other camps who couldn't visit.
Who they couldn't visit.

Just past where
the mountains close in
past Hope.

Not a town but a field
(1 200 acres) leased ($500/month)
and filled with shacks (347, 14 x 25)
built by those who'd live there
in rows called avenues with addresses
for mail, first Opened by Examiner.

From above, rows of shacks (shiplap lumber,
tarpaper) not unlike barracks,
a diorama, snow and everyone
in coats meant for milder weather.

From above as though someone
    up there. *No barbed wires…*
    no armed guards.

Yellow tape around the playgrounds.

Nothing that is not there.

Snapshots of Dot, Willie or Willy, Emi, Mari,
Hippo, Flo, Kiyo, Shiz, Sach. The gang
as hula dancers or in blackface.

Just past 100 miles from the coast.
Had it happened after metric
would they have been closer?
The mountains immovable.

One bathhouse/656.
A quarter mile wet in winter before sleep.

Morning, the sheets stuck to the beds.
しかたがない

What was allowed:
utensils, pots,
a doll, a violin.
150 pounds/adult, 75/child.

Already the boats
tethered (1 137) within 48 hours
of Pearl Harbour. When place became event.

Already the houses
signed to the Custodian.
Sold unbeknownst to pay for their internment.
They call this liquidation.

THIS IS THE… HOSPITAL AT TASHME

Royal Commissioners investigating… living
conditions found much to admire in the efficient
Tashme hospital. White members…
grouped around the bed of Mrs. Mitsui
Mineoka, who has had
an operation which won't
cost her a dime.

Sharpening shipbuilding tools each night
in Manitoba. Thirty sake bottles hidden
in the boathouse
he'd never get back to.

Now Sunshine Valley.
One of BC's best kept secrets.

One day the rain comes, one day
the sun, one day snow.
When the ponds freeze
the majorettes will skate.

Some of the young still there
anyway eating the wild berries getting
the bad readings.

The berries that measure worst
get sold cheaper for dyes.
The good ones make it out
to Western Europe. Organic.

Eight days afloat on her Stearns and Foster
mattress in a bra
78 years old
42 as a nurse she knew
what she needed a bit
of cheese a few raisins 12 ounces
of water a day figured out
when she left Louisiana at 17
it wasn't race it was money
made it to more shoes than she'd
ever need two full-length
mink coats eight days she waited alone
her six TVs adrift in visions
of renos of hardwood of marble
finally flown north
to Chicago in a muumuu
bare feet no underwear

There are people who make miniatures of ruined libraries with trees in them.
There are people who take photographs of miniatures of ruined libraries.
These are the same people.

The people who spend evenings looking at screens that display photographs
of miniatures of ruined libraries with trees in them know
it could always be worse. Are too lucky for their own good.
What does that mean.
Why must suffering.

LONG EXPOSURE (New Orleans, The Veil Reveals, 2005—)

The levees failed the rooms filled.
No 40 days and nights
people found themselves holding
roof beams in a narrow band of air
or no air or never.

•

Reveals a bed, a conflagration,
shades of ashes.

Dogs floated and cartons
and fridges and sewage and coffee cups.

Cars against houses as if propped by a kid
taken off to pee mid-play against his will.

•

A car under a house.
A house over a car.
A car over a car.

•

He hadn't lived there in years.
Stayed at the Hilton with the press.
Wore and wears a vest
that reeks safari. The trophy is obtained
by entering a doorway. Polidori's
many doors. A room that water's stretched
and shrunk and left. How much
is left, how little gives.

•

The house a box on a lot.
The house is a lot of a mess.
The house has no windows left
no walls to keep out those who like me
want to see how bad it gets.

21 May 2020

P.S. "doomscrolling" appeared for the first time in The Times *yesterday, in an Opinion column about the coronavirus (as noted by the Twitter bot @NYT_first_said)*

•

Reveals the long time his looking took.
No bird calls. Maybe yells from clean-up
crews when there were or rescue if still
a chance. Mostly silence.

•

Blue Bell ice cream. Diet Coke.
A pink dishrack, Ajax, pink-fringed
curtains askew, the pink
trim growing into the shapes
of cedars. He also shot
Beirut, riddled walls.

•

A house on a car.
A house on two cars.
A house on a car and a van.
A yellow house on a car and a van.

•

He didn't cast a shadow. We're alone
in somebody's room.

•

A house inside out.
Weeds reeling out.
Weeds unfeeling.

Chunks of plaster
tangle of what plastic
colander laundry hamper
yellow insulation a thing emerges
a lawnmower the ocean floor
a plush bear with a t-shirt
with a year on it or is it or was.

•

A door, a keyhole, a pinhole, a camera.
The camera takes a shot.
The camera takes a shot, heigh-ho the derry oh.

•

Insulation loose with mildew
slopping over beams. Pages congealed,
the words gone.

•

An intimate place.
Do Not Touch.

Rust on each shirt where a hanger.

•

Displacement in the wake of devastating
struck home. Abandoned a portrait.

The veil reveals profusion: exposes
presence. Forced into catastrophe and suffering.

Irresistible a metaphor
to death. A conflict between effect and beauty.

How does the real interact.
Perception leaves a skeleton.

Abandonment witnesses ruins,
stagnant plastic private strangeness.

Charged with the flood, random
interior exile followed.

•

He chose where to stand.
Where to look. Reveals

where he set the edges. The exposure
went in his lungs to live forever.

—Take a picture here. Take a souvenir.

28 March 2020

—It's the end of the world as we know it…
Michael Stipe singing *No time for love like now*
locked down eyes into each of us.

The baby was in me but on the screen
her heart flashed and when I flew
across the country she waited
in the room we were making for her.

SHELTER OBJECT (BC, Sarcophagus, 1986—)

Vancouver sang "Something's Happening
Here." The prince and princess opened
65 pavilions, a highway
of stalled vehicles, an alabaster statue
behind glass. The city had arrived.

•

Gorbachenko suffered a radiation
burn on his back where Sashenok's hand
helped carry him out.

Vomiting and losing
consciousness. Pins and needles,
a taste of metal.

•

41 international +

7 provincial +

2 territorial +

3 state +

9 corporate +

2 theme +

1 special (treasures
from the life of a pharaoh).

•

Just before it happened and before
it opened, Gram died
and there were sandwiches.

•

Scavengers strip all metals.
Visitors ditch protective garments
at set intervals.
More horses than ever.

Google Earth, a place of rivers.

•

She'd have remembered when they found
another pharaoh's tomb. (The curse
of the mosquito, wonderful things.)

Though she didn't know she'd be gone
before Expo opened just
three kilometres away, she hadn't
planned to go. Arthritis,
too many steps.

•

The man with the hand on his back.

The glass roof, fallen in installments.

Her kitchen print of Jesus.

The shut-up air that held the meddled relics.

The land plaza, the air plaza.

The pavilion called USSR.

Near her ear, that purple spot.

Kaput.

The office with its cubicles?
J.C. Penney, Nieman Marcus.
Richmond Night Market?
The dance strangers used to do
when passing in a crowd.
Buffets, choral singing?
Coachella? Glastonbury?
Escape rooms!

•

Her death, the last turn
of the turnstiles, not disasters.

Five years later, the princess
visited Chernobyl's children, listened,
stroked their cancers. Click to see her
lean her chin on her hand. Even thinner
than at Expo where she fainted.

•

Twenties set aside inside
a granddaughter card in one of many drawers,
enough for an ankh, Egyptian symbol
of eternal life. Sixteen, trying on irony
or was it hope.

•

As for the #4 reactor, we estimate
it will be 20,000 years before the real estate
will be fully safe.

•

Her house brought in thousands
less than Asking.
The adjoining lot
of dandelions, next to
nothing.

It all started after Expo
they say. The skyline
filled with cranes.

•

Her last steps up the steps.
Back from dinner for her 87th.

No she was not in bed,
she had gotten up,
the bathroom was a small room, hardly
large enough to fall,
though she must.

The heart of course.

•

A whole new city. They had to
clean the soil first, of industry,
before they built
the glass towers.

•

The lone and level sands.

•

Someone on Facebook has her name.

Meanwhile the trees. It cannot be said often enough
how many leaves. Yesterday a cloud
in the shape of wind the girl M said and a cloud in the shape
of the inside of a fish.
    That you would give me gloves of the skin of a fish.

"Morning on the Guitar."
She wrote that for her daughter.
    Later than either of us
    can know. Just weeks
after cancer took her, lightning.
The girl thought it was safe to stand on the wet grass.

First she croaked she didn't know
why her voice and then a machine was her voice and then
a cane then a bed and no words blinks
less for nearly ten years nearly
nothing. TV a shaken can
of lunch tubed to her gut.
When she chose life did she choose
this life?

In the dream where nothing's left
is freedom. I hold more
than I can.

The cop clutching a stack of DVDs
near the smashed Walmart,
a story illegible.

The night sky the highway
on-ramp heat cast up
on the prisoners the badges the guns.

Remember if your host doesn't look at you
she doesn't see you and you don't
see her either.

KATRINA (Houston, Astrodome, 2005)

At one point life begins. Say it's today.
Say she waits in line and in time
a bus takes her far into the north
of this city she's never seen
beyond the stadium and those waiting
for her don't look at her and burrow
in their forms and it looks like a hotel this place
a pool a basketball court the jackpot
and when finally they come to her
they ask about evictions and police
records and this is not her place.

The bus waits. In the next place
the people are from another country. She knows
her name is the kind white people don't hire
those girls look into their forms
as if in that paper their saviour. This place
looks criminal. She doesn't want her kids
with their kids, gets back on the bus.

Some other person lived the birdsong
mornings the front steps the rattle
of bottles the music the gunshots the porch
evenings the flood rising
the roof still in place getting closer the axe
she'd stashed just in case so lucky
to be saved she thought she was saved.

There are bins here for trash there are toys
for the kids there are tables of leaflets of places
to go two jobs and a house
and a school in Colorado but she'd freeze to death.

Is it still there her house what floats
in the water if the water's still there who's there
in her stuff someone's been there someone
sprayed a cross to tell what they found and when
a man with a camera comes it's not like she
knows it's not like he asks. She can't
know this she'll never see the photographs
she can't remember the smell of the backyard
magnolia this must be what dying's like.

He steps where she won't
step again and looks at what
was left and it is not good and enough
light makes its way through the stiff
curtains for the eye of his camera to open and
take everything and leave it there and leave.

Then life begins.
Someone will carry armfuls
to the curb of what's left
some student volunteer on spring break
in some classroom she learned a poem
about rivers she could still say she could
almost she can almost remember.

That man with grains
of earth in his hands. —*Some day*
I'm going to build on it.

She grew up thinking the radio always played
music from where you came from.

Where did she go those hours alone in the tower watching for fire.
Where when nowhere and the glass and the walls and the forest
and the cells that make the edges and the edges of the cells and how far
in is far and where does she go when she's that far in
where does she write with a toothbrush
where does the girl hide in that room
all those years where he comes in
and he comes in where
is the farthest
hardest part.

Early on in the end of the world
it hit me there would still be hurricanes
and fire still flood and how could that be
and it was and it was not the end of the world
but it was 4.1 million acres of California 10 000
buildings 31 people worst on record so far.

Let it go is what they say to make you small.

Some say everyone lost someone.
Can we say some could afford to be lucky?

INTERIOR (BC, しかたがない, 1941—)

The cenotaph my parents, my brother,
and I used to pass those rare days
in Stanley Park, I knew only as
The War. Not far
from the miniature train and near
the cherry blossoms.

1941: *The light atop the Japanese Canadian War Memorial*
is extinguished.

Look at Slocan look at these places
in the Interior too many
people to see how
empty it was. Though my parents
were infants they say there are things
I can't understand.

Where did they come from, where
did they go? That is the story
we wish to know.

From *Dinosaurs: A Little Golden Book.*
From a pangolin, no a bat.
Later from a mink perhaps?
To the tigers in the Bronx, to a cat.
Could the mice in the basement?
Could a lab?

In Houston the crime rate did not go up
after the NOLA folks came.

TASTE THE UNTOUCHED.
FEEL THE UNKNOWN.
SEE THE WILD.

A certificate to state your dose.

$5—$9 USD gets you an *ecologically-*
clean dinner in a Chernobyl state
canteen (vegetarian upon request.)
During two days… the human body
receives a radiation dose… less than
500 whole body x-ray screenings.

LONG EXPOSURE (New Orleans, Weather, 2005—)

It is not that it is difficult to look at.
It is not that difficult to look at.
There is a bed.
There is a substance, erroneous.
Weather brought it.
Weather is not our friend.

Whether or not.
It happens.
Without regard.
Where a bed was, this.

•

Houston Dallas San Antonio Baton
Rouge Lafayette Denver Detroit.
When does temporary stop?

•

Get out of here the wind will blow
your house down. The wolf
has come for your children.

•

Only what's metallic.
Only what's ceramic.
Water eats the rest.

—And we do not want them back when the war ends, either.

They shut the housing projects though they'd survived
the storm it was time there was lead there were gangs.

They fired the teachers they'd been nothing
but a pain in the ass.

They put the courses online they'd been dreaming it for years.
Private schools already on track, each kid with a tablet.

Seventy pages to apply for money
for a new house.

Midterm, they said rethink multiple low-stakes assignments,
recorded classes anytime, anywhere.

The program called The Road Home.

Added a mental health hub to the website.

Pack up your troubles in your old kit-bag
and smile smile smile.

WAVE (Tōhoku, Saw, 2011—)

Saw a fallen man saw
boots in a doorway
a shop of candies in pink

packages on shelves beside faux silk cherry
blossoms in vases for spring.

—I had only heard something like that once
before: in Chernobyl.
Total silence.

Late March, photographs of noon
around the world unpeopled.
Each photographer's small shadow at their feet.

A myth. Workers settlers tourists
the dogs that came from the dogs left behind.

A bowl of intact oranges.
Each of the candies in the package in a package.

A body stuck in mud
face down in mud.

The girl stood in a line when the wave came
they'd been told to stand in a line
safe from the school that could fall as the teachers
argued whether the hill behind the school or the higher
ground near the bridge or the traffic circle or
stay here as the manual said and the wave
came like a hunger engulfing.

Her mother learned to operate machinery
to excavate. When the girl's body
was found some miles off
the head was not there. Her mother kept digging.

When the deed is water
when half the names are dead when a great-great
built it no insurance when the insurance gives
$400 after 50 years of payments when the shoddy
sheetrock from China has to be ripped out when
the contractor takes off with the cash.

1 000 000 000 tons of waste
water to be released
into the sea ten years after the disaster.
A realistic solution... gradual, trial...
could start in 2 years
40 years to complete

1988: Redress:
the government apologizes. The light
atop the war memorial flares back.

That's when she lost it. Prom dress
flood-lined in the closet. Sludge
lines on the bus shelters along Canal. Then
new palm trees for the tourists. $35K a pop.

Probably 80% client base victims of contractor fraud.
80% city underwater.

It could happen to you.

If the first claim was for Heart

Attack or Stroke, second event coverage will

be provided for Life-Threatening Cancer. If the first

claim was for Life-Threatening Cancer, second

event coverage will be provided for Heart Attack. If

the first claim was for a critical

illness other than Heart Attack, Life-

Threatening Cancer or Stroke, no

coverage is provided under this rider.

Particulate on plastic clamshells of salac
in the breath on the bu
in the corridors of hospital or powe
on the flowers for a birthday
the candle the wish

Old walls of barge board still stand.
Seasoned by years on the river.
Willows at the base of levees do the trick.

April 202C

Those who say we forgot the Spanish flu
weren't there.
The man whose twin succumbed in infancy
now coughs his diagnosis.
—*We could have been much better prepared for this.*

LONG EXPOSURE (New Orleans, Trace, 2011)

Best Coffee-Table Books 2011 - The Daily BeastLooking for a last-minute gift? Here ;s our roundup of the best books of the year that will look mighty fine on a coffee table near you. Lush Bella: havana through the lens of robert polidori havana through the lens of robert polidori . Robert Polidori ;s Havana | Man Make Home Robert Polidori ;s Havana . While some aesthetes may prefer viewing an image in its . these rooms are interesting to me for . As we meet up at his first solo exhibition in . Robert Polidori - Time Out Hong Kong. . polis: Featured Artist: Robert Polidori Featured Artist: Robert Polidori . It is filed under Icons, illustrations, photographs and tagged with Havana , Robert Polidori , Versailles. Best Books of 2011. The Nourse shares a similar history of fascinating performers like Jim Morrison and . Robert Polidori - Grey not Grey Robert Polidori is an American photographer born in Montreal, Canada, who lives between Paris and New York. Download Robert Polidori : Parcours Museologique Revisite Robert Polidori – Wikipedia, the free encyclopedia Robert Polidori (born 1951 in Montreal,. [via]. . Simple, elegantly beautiful and sad at the same time. Robert Polidori : Havana » Blog Archive » Cheap Stephen Shore . On the surface his subjects are buildings, but at the core his lens is . Book summary: Robert Polidori's Havana is a haunting city of sherbet colors and peeling stucco, grand colonial architecture in decay, and real people who hang their

•

There's a look he needs
the room to give it won't
if anyone's in it.

•

It's biblical. Fills a quarter of my desk,
half if open, weighs a quarter of my desk
maybe, the caps AFTER THE FLOOD
the colour of the worn
steps of the double shotgun cottages.

M wished for someone
who knew everything so she could know
if there was another life
because if she let me put the sticker
on the organ donor card she might be
missing an arm and she wouldn't want
to be missing an arm. I asked
if she'd need her body
if there were another life she said
yes. She asked if there was
another life I said I didn't think so.

In the margins: *Residential Jungle Gyms*

Birthday at the Labyrinth

Create your own world

Free to Play RPG in Hell

Play free girl games

M says *Why are the people from olden times*
dead? I want to meet Jesus.

—*Your grand-maman is old.*
Then she'll be dead.

KATRINA (New Orleans, Cash, 2005—)

Fats was said to fan himself
with $1 000 bills. Travel with his own
pots and pans and fear
other food. Missing three days
got lifted out his next album
Alive and Kickin'.

The house
on all the tours.

A double shotgun model.
Half for him and his studio
half for his wife and kids.

•

18 to 20 hour days shovelling *heartbreaking wet stuff*

•

Passed 'round and 'round she said
(from a park where told to spend her days
the homeless shelter shut till dusk her voucher
for the disaster shelter stolen) *like a bag of snacks*
at a Super Bowl party.   A separate bowl of chips per household.

•

The brilliant swirl
of daiquiris returned.

Home Depot St. Bernard Parish
for at least a year said to be the top seller
in the entire U. S. of A.

•

No tinsel that first winter.
You had to order it
or imagine.

•

Finally got your trailer
then the nosebleeds
the nights you'd wake
gasping. The formaldehyde the bad
tests the lack
of recompense.

WE BUY HOUSES Cash Fast!
Eleven years later the signs still there.

A few years after four years
in labour camps someone found him
at a wedding in L.A. Not an actor.
All actors killed by the Khmer Rouge. He didn't
want the part. Fled the set when it felt
true. Born 1940 like Lennon. Dying
in labour his wife hadn't asked for him
though he specialized in obstetrics. All doctors
killed. He won an Oscar. His character
died of pancreatic cancer. —*My heart*
is satisfied. I have done something
perfect. His Oscar rubbed free of gold

found by his niece after. Shot
in the garage or in the driveway
near his BMW. Foiled
robbery maybe. No will. Part two
opens with the twin towers. He said
The Killing Fields was not real enough.

Rail cars full of oil slid faster down
the slope until at the curve where the town
was a birthday party exploded and a woman
with cancer who'd chosen not to mark
this year still lives because she didn't
go. All that long-dead
plankton lit the sky.

Am I the happy loss
Will I still recoil
When the skin is lost

Am I the worthy cross
Will I still be soiled
When the dirt is off

Echo and the Bunnymen tix on sale
22 July 2020 for 11 June 2021.
(Check back in 2021 all dates 2022.
Check 2022 happening!
Original tickets remain valid.)

SHELTER OBJECT (Zone, Stalker, 1979—)

In the film before it happened
there is no answer there is no question.

What you wish for's better left unknown.
The water they lie in flotsam and fishes.

When they enter the Zone there's colour.
Each leaf interrogates.

It's never easy in a place of colour.
Stalker's job is to walk them through.

For men a place of freedom. Far enough
inside the self there is no self outside.

His wife tells the lens she could not
have lived a different life.

She covers him with a jacket. While he sleeps
their daughter moves glasses with her mind.

Downstream from a chemical plant it seeped
their deaths into them. They met it in reflections.

You can't go back the way you came.
Next time will be different.

He walks by several times
each day in windchill in swelter
the same warm coat head bent forward
sometimes with a spray bottle cooling his face
I can't hear what he says.

Not a place but a print.
Not a wall but a frame.
Not a place but a state.
Not an ode but a mood.
Not a dog but a dirge.
Not a bone.

What you forget
won't be missed. What you'll wish
you'd kept can't be guessed. No way
to avoid disappointment even if
you book now.

It snows and snows she says *Never*
to get lost is not to live, not to know
how to get lost brings you
to destruction.

Google solnit covid there she is
I knew she would be there to say
it's okay people are good.

TASHME (BC, Tashimi, 1942—)

Delivered in secret in snow,
soy sauce rations.
The barrels a gift from Japan
some wanted to refuse.

Digging for a basement to store vegetables
a father and son found pipes and presto
change-o: running water
in the kitchen! A bath
without the wet trek back!
The father started a *shōyu* factory
at the camp. Later the son became
an engineer.

If you're on a boil advisory for years
do you still wash your hands to Happy Birthday?

(Most men already taken
to build the Hope-Princeton
highway generations would drive to vacations.)

May Day picnics, kindergarten,
weddings, births.
Cooking classes. Judo. Church
and Sunday school, Christian
and Buddhist. Boy Scouts,
Tashme Stars. A banner:
1ST TASHME TROOP. Be Prepared.

Eventually the farewell dinner of the nurses.

Fifty years later the reunion
as though another kind of camp.

Tashimi written on the back of a photo
as though a word. As though Japanese.

Upheaval meaning the earth moved.
Unrest meaning no one slept.

She knew which bus, how to
make it up the hill home. That house that spread its ocean
view around itself resplendent as a mane.
That house built by oil through
the mountains. Then she couldn't say
which bus. Then a facility, a door
that wouldn't open.

M said before she was born
she waited at the Kids' Museum.

KATRINA (New Orleans, Camellia Grill, 2002—)

The man who sang "Swing Low" as he whipped up omelettes
knew he was a show. At first he meant it. It was
easy. Then he watched a mother's eyes

go dead and the ground that was not solid
open. But she was ashes. The ground was in the song. The song
was morning and night. He watched a child veer into the street
on a bike. The song was evening. He watched the dollars pile up
smaller each time, the rent higher, and then the swirl
on the screen then the wind and the rain then the water.

After, they loved the song more, it was their grief
he was singing, the idea of the grief
of those who missed a city they'd never seen.

He stayed for the song and the froth of the egg, for the oily spray,
the wash across the pan, how quick it was done and tossed
on a plate, oval and blue for a retro allure,
with slathered wet toast at the counter.

He's still at it. One day the song will be another's
and he'll drop in from his house down the street
from where he grew up. No, he'll move
to his girl's place in Kansas, he'll drop at a crosswalk,
get shot at, get locked up for who he looked at
wrong or not and for his last
he'll ask for an omelette. But last meals
aren't a thing anymore down there. That's why
they come for the song.

When she was not there in the sand and not there
on the slide and not
there was a film in which everything ended.
A car pulled out of the lot

and it was too late all
over while we'd talked, my friend's girls
nearby mine cupping sand
through her fingers until where?
Meanwhile no one who'd been watching
who'd noticed my eyes not on her
lunged to take her hand and lead her off.
She'd passed the splash pad the sand pit
the fish slide all the way to the red
tunnel she didn't understand my face
        said *But I was here* and kept playing.

Her favourite's the maple tree
because it saves us. Where we meet
if fire.

In the virus spring the leaves come slow.
It's cold.
She needs me there to fall asleep.
If not she thinks of fire.
Her books still at school, burning.
Our house on fire, her phone saved to call 911.

In her dream her sister played in the park
without her. Now she doesn't want to go
to the park at daycare because her sister
might be there and play in the park
without her.

Suffering in the eye of the beholder.

An episode of *The Twilight Zone*.

So fast you turned away from one
to help the other to the roof the small hand
gone. Swirling somewhere down in that water.
How many times her hand gone from that cooler
you held onto and you called God and there
she was again bobbing.

AT THE END (Pointe-Claire, If I Were, 2011—)

If I were to go now, like this, my head forward into the screen,
the girl in the crib would cry a long time.
The older girl at daycare until the last friend left and no one
would come and late charges accrue and the teacher would call
home and no answer and cell and no
answer and his cell and voicemail
he wouldn't check and the grandparents' machine would be full
and she would stay with the girl.
The baby asleep again by then, the crib rail chewed, a smell of diaper and hunger.
Her breaths on the monitor the minotaur.
The garbage can emptied by the curb, the driveway empty, the car
still at the garage, the bill unpaid, a bag of flyers on the steps
dusted in snow, the mail in the vestibule where it fell.
The teacher calling the numbers again.
The teacher driving by the house with the girl in her daughter's car seat.
Her daughter with a sitter who kept calling.
The teacher ringing the bell, waking the baby to wails.
The house otherwise still.
The teacher calling 911.
The sirens of fire, ambulance, police, whoever first.
The door broken down.
Someone entering.

Someone calling.
Someone finding the baby.
The girl crying the teacher holding the girl.
Holding back the girl.
Someone finding.
My body leaning as though aspiring.
Maybe I leaned into a pain
that was strange and thought
I will be gone and
was gone. The screen black.
Touched awake, the screen flashing
lines written before the instant of ending.
The girl screaming, would she be screaming,
would she be still, the baby wailing, someone
calling and calling and no one
answering. Their father back on the late train.
The teacher still holding.
The body by then body.
The teacher turning away.
The three of them holding.
Days of holding the three of them forging.
Days of the screen and the room
with the screen and a silence.
The French door always closed.
The younger beginning forgetting.
The older beginning remembering.
The one and the other unhinging.
In time the door opening the screen awakening.
The older watching mermaids.
The younger upstairs with her father playing.
The older learning to water the plants
in the high windows, remembering Christmas
when the card with the blue metallic dove.
It will stay on the sill for years
or the blue bin or the green
or the garbage.

If everything's important nothing is. He says.
Everything's important. She says.

Carried from Tut's tomb –
statues on stretchers.

Once the most beloved:
the woman at the checkout with a pack of mock chicken and a can of peas.
The man dead in his bath at the residence, his skin seared
he couldn't get out. Prisoner dead in the shower.

The uncle dead at the grand piano reading his paper
in the house of his dead parents, his mother's brushes
still on the vanity, the dust, the phone
in the entry hall ringing.

We are each. At the toilet in the night.
In the bed in the shared room,
the other looking out the window at the blue mountains.

NO WAVE (Fukushima, Shelter, 2011)

No water here, no need
to run. What came
couldn't be seen. The particles. What
made the lights come on.
The cleaner choice.

Which brings worse
shame: the photographs of disorder
in the homes or order
in the shelters? Which sadness is greater.

Here are days without seasons.
In a warehouse, a trailer.
A cardboard box with a window cut out.

Sleep passes time, dried flowers
gather safer dust. Heaps: newspaper, ribbons,
cords, glue, balloons, sleep. Shoes
at the entrance say home.

A woman and her mother
live where forbidden, so the elder, who cannot
remember anything, won't have to forget.

孤独死

Others would go back if allowed
even if death. If only running water. If only power.

One has forgotten her backpack.
One lost a snack. Neither of the touch
screens work. Somebody wants to walk
in the aisle. Someone wants the oxygen
masks to come down. There's one extra
per row but what if there are many
babies? The slide won't open
if there's no water. The life vests are not
party favours. One is agile enough
to crouch down and see.

A shape on the floor in the dark.
Morning, the peanut butter's gone.
A heap of seeds meant for birds
spewing from a bitten gap
in the plastic. Sweep
the shells and seed-
black shit. The traps
that let them live
don't work.

New slivers of shit each morning.
Twelve years since last time.
First wrappers of granola bars bitten to tinsel,
bags of chocolate chips, then Ryvita, Kamut Krisp,
then Styrofoam Easter eggs, soap, plasticine crafts.
Old goldfish food we forgot.
Cross-hatchings of gnashing.

When told there's a thing that can happen
to your body that shuts your mouth and stops
your arms that makes you stay in bed

she laughed at first. Said But what. No one
stays in bed all the time. Then her face
gone a while. How do they get
better? We talked about
something else.

LONG EXPOSURE (New Orleans, Stuff, 2005—)

That with which a house is filled the filling
the colours gone the essence
distinctions screens and tubs chairs shelves
lampshadesbooks and clothes and rugs hauled out
and tossed with what mask with what face
with what voice with what breath. Who took the things
from here to there and left them and who took them
away and with what face and to what place.

•

food waste (raw, cooked or spoiled), fruits and vegetables fish, seafood, meat, eggs (including shells and bones) dairy products, bread, cereals, pasta, coffee grounds and filters, tea bags, corn cobs and husks, nuts and shells, etc. cakes, sweets and flour grass clippings (free of herbicides and insecticides) garden waste (flowers, fruits, plants and weeds) bark, wood chips, sawdust and straw leaves, twigs and conifer needles bundles of branches under 1 metre (3 ft. 3 in.) in length, maximum diameter of branches 5 cm (2 in.), and small tree roots corks human and animal hair, feathers cold untreated wood ash soiled paper and cardboard (tissues, paper towels, pizza boxes, paper napkins, fries containers, etc.) domestic animal litter (without excrement)

•

What shapes here what things
what inventory is each thing a thing or part of.
What is the shirt the tangle of jewellery the golf ball the blanket
warm in winter the folding metal chair for guests a mess of rust
the folded stroller the yard of things the life
of things the bike the bowl the death of
things the opened couch the fibreglass.

•

The morning after.

•

In his eighties, bent from years
of violin, years of reading, the neighbour
fishes the Ziploc that dropped
when the blue truck's arm grabbed
the blue bin and shook and shook,
out of the puddle. It troubles him
to see it there. The effort
less than of doing nothing.

Late winter, a nephew maybe
of the new neighbour from Shanghai
bounces a basketball alone each day.
Spring, the neighbour (P.J. he says)
waters his grass seed daily.
When I ask how he's doing he wavers his hand
okay, not great,
he says *Manger, dormir, manger, dormir.*

•

How small
could you get and still be
there how much
could your stuff swell
to become nothing.

How could a house have held
more than its size
like a clown car like that African clawed frog
in the bag in the car
on the way home from the mall who vomited
a mess of brine shrimp I thought were guts.

Alive in the tank
38 years later.

Restrictions lift.
A weight in the live trap.
He drives the mouse to a field
near a cinema near a forest.

Later another.
Later a groundhog.
Another groundhog.
A skunk!
We put the trap away.
The hole dug beside the foundation,
who knows how far.

•

The more unique the contents the lower
the income is what he said.

•

I might tell from the name
who lived there
but there are no names.

A chair in a beautiful space, no matter
how beautiful the chair is, can never be
as beautiful to me as the plain space.

One hundred days after the apocalypse he followed the footsteps
in the snow from the hotel of the dead to the airport
of the living. Until he saw them he'd thought
he was the only one.

Snow makes time visible.
By the end of the day the car's
a mound. The steps a slope.
The man who lies down
just a moment.

SANDON (BC, So Dark, 1942—)

That first winter 100 froze.
Not a round number.

•

20 000 visitors a year.
A few residents.
Fleet of trolley buses.
No name on the map for the road.

•

So deep it's not a valley
it's a gorge. Dark early
even summertime.

So narrow they built the street
right over the creek.

•

Many theatres and opera houses,

a soft drink plant, a cigar factory, 3

sawmills, 3 churches, 2 newspapers,

a schoolhouse, a hospital.

Miners and millionaires, con men

and gamblers, land speculators and 'ladies

of the evening.'

•

Sometimes someone chooses
a use for the empty.
Ghosts are not.

•

At least 100 miles inland?
Check. Rooms with no one
in them? Check. Let
the trains come.

•

Snow higher than the roofs.
Doukhobors brought vegetables.

•

Enemy aliens.
Mostly Buddhists.

In the photograph of the funeral
flowers from somewhere.
As many as the snow is deep.

•

Is there a plaque?
How many came how many
left there is no math.

•

No sign of the sea
or the boats or the coast
that was theirs when
the boats were.

Had the army corps of engineers
not failed.

Once more with feeling.

The levees needed T-walls not Is
needed good hard clay.

Wave action reduced them
to the pile of sand they were.

The stink of the pail. Morning,
diapers dragged to the curb,
licked clean by raccoons.

Cardboard in three months, wood in up to three years, a pair of wool socks in up to five. A plastic shopping bag may take 20 years; a plastic cup, 50… An aluminum can is with us for 200 years, a glass bottle for 500, a plastic bottle for 700, and a Styrofoam container for a millennium.

E says *When I'm dead I don't want people to take off my hair to make perruques for people with cancer.*

SHELTER OBJECT (Chernobyl, New Safe Confinement, 2017)

They looked close and saw they were sore afraid.
Couldn't face it near enough to fix it.
Couldn't not or all hell.

They made a plan to plan.
Designated 12 and they chose.
To be constructed near enough to put it
into place, far enough to not get sick.
Eighteen ships 2 500 trucks
parts from Italy. Thousands
working other thousands living in that zone
called exclusion.

Robots built inside it
to finish the dismantling
then cease and stew in their fumes.
The worst sealed in.

On the steel roof a clean shine
overcast sky and shadows
of machinery. Inside might be Mars.

The children's organs grew
outside their bodies the cows' descendants
ate the grass and lived and died and lived. You'd think

Metal 5 days
Glass up to 5 days
Ceramics 5 days
Wood 4 days
Plastics, stainless steel 2 to 3 days
Cardboard 24 hours
Aluminum 2 to 8 hours
Copper 4 hours
Paper from a few minutes to 5 days
depending on the strain

Whoops… it's airborne.

the consequences would be more visible the dying more
dire you'd think a plume of fire would rise
but this is no ordinary dragon. Its spell quiets
this world this beauty men who've left
long for all their days saving the world
from the place they long for.

One hundred years they say it'll last.
A new team needs to get to work on after.

She tried her way through the bricks.
There was time for that. Time
for a child to be the size of a pinkie nail
then a palm then a fist then a head
the size of a fist. Running
circles around that universe.
Then whatever talk got let in.
A will sharp enough to wedge
up a floorboard. Someone down there
must hear and have feigned not hearing
a long time now. Signals out windows
where there were windows. The mind
shrinks to a walnut someone
said the mind summons itself says
        Hello, fancy meeting you
        in a purple stew, just like its mother
used to say. There's an echo in here.
The mind is the size of the nearly fluorescent
bloom on a sensitive plant, which resembles
the ball that is Horton's treasure from which come
yeps enough to mean lives and finally

We are here! and world
saved awhile. Who knows what
on one's lashes. To live
all those years knowing yourself lost,
mourned, knowing no one
still looking. Could you forge a rope
from the will to not endure?

Photographs of land mines are beautiful.
Land mines are beautiful.
Meaning to the eye.
If such suspension possible.
The colours resemble the minerals on canisters of ash
of the dead in a long-gone asylum.
Two friends who don't know each other
sent me these links the same day. I send them
http://www.lorinix.net/the-city/
so we can all see the miniature library
abandoned to eternity.

He started out photographing
apartments of the recently
deceased. The one who could object
is out of the picture.
Get it?

They are singular, not They. They are
You though not you or maybe you yes you
you and you and you
are me are not me I am not me.

From the FEMA trailer lot on some outskirts
there's a shuttle to Walmart.
At dusk the sky golds up.

Zone meaning you need boots you need pants (no leggings! no shorts!) you need insurance you need a passport you will see a self-settler you will see the town of Pripyat formerly of 50 000 you will spend all day there you will be dosed less than you fear more than you hope you will cycle over the St. Claude Avenue Bridge toward the sustainable Brad Pitt houses the potholes the weed growth the gas station corner store with po'boys shrimp fried rice you may fear shots you may feel wrong whatever you take cannot be measured but you will be measured.

Later, some trailers went up for auction
dirt cheap. Stickers *Not to be used*
for housing scraped off.
Filling lots in North Dakota
oil boomtowns 10 years later.
Seven to a trailer.
One guy lived in one in NOLA
moved out here to make a buck and found
himself in one again.

Who will you be seen by in that room
that sees nothing that is itself in winter
as in spring that does not breathe that does
not feel that is a room that took the place
of space that filled a wish that filled a patch
of earth and made it bigger by ending it
with edges that made it wider
with windows gave it body by trespassing
on its body with a backhoe
with concrete with two-by-fours
and slats of sanded oak and green
carpet woven in a factory that does not
run on human hands.

She does her 10 000 steps within those walls
just steps from the ocean.

LONG EXPOSURE (New Orleans, Man with Camera, 2005—)

The man with the camera
had means. Paid for his ticket out of pocket
paid for the film went where what
he saw was almost more than he
could bear he kept looking.

Where people had tried to find
their photographs where they'd come
and cried and puked and torn through
seeking he came and opened the aperture
a long time the old way.

What he found he didn't say. He saw.

Dared think himself invisible
not mortal could not lose everything.

•

Some say he looted.

•

Auctions of the prints show up often
on Google Alerts but that's another's profit.

The cameras the prints he paid to make.
10% of proceeds from the book donated.

But 90%. But the publisher's cut.
But he could afford.

But I can afford.
The art of arrangement an eloquence.

•

To look at what he's looked at
the practice of adults. A child
would know better.

•

The involuntary vomiting
gets tiring he said. He seems the type
to walk out of a restaurant
if poorly served or disappointed
quietly take
offense if expectations are not met.
Those hours wading,
waiting, those weeks
alone with the dead and the wrecked.

He says *I'm not getting as much done*
as I used to at the studio.
He says *I'm starting to miss people in restaurants.*
His concepts for survival: acceptance. Ego-reduction.

He listened
to music in this city, he didn't live
in this ward but he lived
in this city, here's his photo
as a teen, Brother
Martin High School, 1964.

•

Some came back. Had forms to fill got
hammers and saws had hands.

•

We're aftermath, me in a room
he puts me in, no, I
stand in and he takes the picture.

No, makes, his word,
mine, it's my
mind we're in.

In the dream he lives
here. Where I live's
not clear. The walls' story's
someone else's. He's like
in the interviews, mostly
silent, an edge, I get
what he's saying.

•

A body wrapped on a mattress
and a stack of newspapers and a lampshade
he stood there and took as long
as it took and left and that
was that.

•

—But as soon as I put the camera
down and look away, I'm
frightened. It's the weirdest thing.

Dug up buried trucks sold the metals
sometimes tested sometimes seized
sometimes out in the world leaking.

M says *She says we can see*
all kinds of things if we
close our eyes but
that's not true.

Over a million watched the full movie of the 2004 tsunami.
Taken down after a copyright claim, up again
(nearly two million views), gone again,
back, URL keeps changing, *THIS VIDEO MAY BE*
INAPPROPRIATE FOR SOME USERS. I understand
and wish to proceed. In 72 minutes
one could conceive a child, make a cake,
let bread rise, wait in line for bread, walk this far, run that far,
cycle farther, do a big shop, have a long coffee, wait
by a subway entrance to collect enough change
for a coffee, work a fraction of a shift, brunch,
watch a bunch of *Schoolhouse Rocks*, listen
to *Lolita Nation* in almost its entirety, watch all but the last
24 minutes of *Manhattan*, decide
to boycott *Manhattan*, fly
to Manhattan, hitchhike wherever, install a door,
start a novel, repeat
a word so often it loses meaning.

TASHME (BC, Sunshine Valley, 1970—)

A playground a barn some silos
vaguely nuclear. A museum on Facebook

open Saturdays or by appointment.
Do all the lost places

Mid-May they add a virtual tour.
Now because you can't go there you can go there.

fall to the bottom of our pockets?
When I looked up the museum I learned

        my friend was dying. *To keep you connected,*
        each cabin includes free WIFI for up to two

        devices. Most come not knowing
what it is. A row of cabins

        for non-campers. *You may have a difficult time*
        leaving the comfort of this unique accommodation

        experience. Mostly an expanse. Rows
of trailers. Thin rows of cedars.

How alike the rows the shadows.

When asked where she came from
        E says *My mummy's tummy.*

The suburban lot that's left
of my great-grandparents' two acres
went for $1.7 million. A tear-down. Gravenstein apple
and the pear tree forming useless fruit.

Beswick horses for my daughters. A Ziploc of shells.

If my cousins toss their mother's photo albums
she'll haunt them, that's what she said.

From us it passes on when we pass on.
Mostly women.

Used to be executrix, executor. These days
the one who does the distribution's
a liquidator.

Her older daughter chose to keep some of her blouses.
When seven weeks later her younger daughter flamed up
in her own box of loss, she wore green pants
she was making herself, the waistband unfinished.

LONG EXPOSURE (Home, Slipcase, 2005—)

It is beauty it is a surfeit it is a violence the presentation of which in this form is almost is sometimes repulsive is the result of much care of thousands of hours of suffering of thousands of dollars of flights of carbon emissions of eyes of lives as I sit by a window on a sunny chill November morning the morning of my daughter's birthday I could walk through the woods I could trim the hydrangea I am looking at these photos. I am bored I am moved I have marked a page for years with an ad for a foundation expert. I finish after I have been there. I have seen these houses or where they were. There they are on Google there he is on YouTube talking about how to sequence a book of photographs. He says they are not about the people. There is a story in chronology not about recovery. At the end cypresses. At the end water. At the end proceeds donated to rebuilding New Orleans' music culture and to a Jazz & Heritage Station. He lives in California.

•

Voices from Chernobyl fits in my purse.

The author not the author yes
the author left Belarus in 2000 for sanctuary in Paris,
Gothenburg, Berlin. In 2011 returned to Minsk
where she keeps a modest apartment.

He went looking she went asking
she went listening. She wanted
to be a bowl but was a funnel.

She wanted to be a funnel.
She got a prize for it, one of the biggest.

Who do they think they are and me
on their backs like a monkey not even winged.

•

The name was retired.
Katia took its place.

•

He stopped after that.
—*New Orleans, that's the most depressing one.*

He chose instead to go where people chose
how to build how they lived.

Brits went to the colonies Caribbeans came
from the colonies. Mostly not the same colonies.
The same row of southeast London brick houses
Gram left forever at 13.

If you lived here
you'd be home now.

SHELTER OBJECT (Chernobyl, Elena's Hair, 1986—)

The shield, called "Pyatachok"
("five kopek coin") before
the disaster, was afterwards named
Component "E" and nicknamed
"Elena"; the twisted
fuel bundles still attached to
it are called "Elena's hair."

Liquidators called the roof Masha the place of greatest
danger they went on dates with her
a timer ticking.

Below lesser Nina and the weakest
Katia, Area K.

Who had the most roentgens.
Whose Geiger counter clicked fastest.

•

All he wanted was to be a fireman. All they told him
was a fire. —*In fourteen days a person dies.*
In a world with giraffes and chandeliers
and fire. His wife bought chocolates for the nurses.

•

Women who spun and knitted
the wool from the Chernobyl sheep
got registered later as liquidators.

I had a self then a child. In another time
my blood would've kept on
running out onto the sheets, an ordinary
death. Or another place. Here,
now (then), a shot
stopped the flow.

Death from childbirth isn't news unless we make it.
It's not as though I died.
An artist cut the sheets into a scroll.
No trace of blood.
The vernissage in February, an edge in the air.

Don't think
of her at 97, the window
onto the bloated lake, the sky
of rust. Someone might visit.
It might be lush. It will be
2107. At the end
she won't be afraid.
After, she'll be dead.

In his dim basement room he says he lies there and eats bread.
Where did the day go?
He will go out on his scooter like a kid he says
he will go out.

You Want It Darker
he wrote for us to
understand after.

In films we go to space to find each other.

LONG EXPOSURE (New Orleans, Address, *bis bis*, 2005—)

My address a caption.
Lookers enthralled by the sage Subaru
crashed through the big window
of the office once the garage
glass and trinkets and books ravaged
to the stipple of sand twin filing cabinets
drawers wedged open where
someone tried to salvage. Downstairs
a slew of unendurable plastic.

May 2020

When the painter lets us in her home
we're breaking the rules.
No one else inside for months.
We stand far from the art and each other.
We are sure we are safe.
We don't say we are almost
in each other's bodies now.

•

That being white etcetera. The neighbourhood
of greatest devastation. The people whose homes.

We thought we'd been so long in our homes.
It was so early we weren't even wearing masks.

•

The man with his mother in the story man without his mother on the screen
mother in her wheelchair with the blanket on her folded forward
in her wheelchair with the blanket with the sheet the poncho his mother
who stopped asking when the bus was coming
and died the bus wasn't coming died and he put her aside with the other dead
as he was told there was no cold for the dead no power days later
when the bus came she was still there. He wanted to go to her
they said Get on the bus. He got on the bus.
Her name his name his cell number on a paper somewhere on her.
Somewhere near her.

M says *What comes after the life?*

—And when everyone's dead?

There will be bone china vases,
cups with flowers at their elbows,
all listed like Christmas and distributed.
I'll still think of her as often.

M says *She's me when I'm*
little and I'll be myself
when I'm older.

If I go back far enough, she will be born.
Then I'll really be there, paying attention.

SHELTER OBJECT (Chernobyl, Readings, 2017—)

When the bar was closing she told me
she went there. Her partner's choice.

On her own she'd never. It was safe
the tour operator took care.

Before me a man read about visiting
a wartorn country. The I was and wasn't.

A way of seeing a worse place
than his depression his friend said.

She lived there. All this way he'd come
to see the danger. She stayed in.

Washed dishes. He read
without looking at us.

A few years later we both showed up
to attend a panel on what we could say

and couldn't and how and who
could decide. We wanted

not to harm. We wanted
(I wanted) to disappear.

There was a day I was not grateful and what happened was terrible.
Rain fell from the sky and I griped.
It turned to ice.
Dogs followed me, biting.
The slick sidewalk held my sagging haunches, too young
to be broken but almost marking the beginning
of the end. Too thrifty for heat, I shivered
enough to anger myself. Or when they said vigour
I heard anger. The cornucopia began to rot, its magnificent shell
made badly of *papier mâché*, a *piñata*
stuffed with warty gourds not meant to eat.
Then the sun came out inside my head. What I had squandered.
The baby slept for hours and what I wrote was glorious
and even though it all was lost in the great crash of the laptop
the happiness lasted.

Superman spun the planet
backward to drag silt from the mouth
of the woman he loved wedged in a slit
in the earth from the big quake.
What gave him the force to turn time
was it love was it rage?

Love is long-suffering.
Eventually, the tantrums will stop altogether.
Hold your child in your arms if possible
without hurting. Wait
for the storm to pass. Designate an area.
Let Yes *mean Yes,*
No, *No. Is God's Kingdom*
a condition of the heart?

LONG EXPOSURE (New Orleans, Remains, 2005—)

The front steps left behind when the barge took the house six blocks.
The mind strains and tears from its backing.
A floater goes off into that vitreous bit forever.
Eventually it'll settle lower in the field.
Eleven years later the steps.

•

Off the coast 50 000 year old cypresses
still smell fresh if cut. Back when folks lived here
they made earth here. Before channels
quickened the route for freight
and made the water salt
they made a place.

•

Soap in a wrap, a sleeve
on the glass, the sheets
new each time he comes back.

Will sleeves come back?
The staff masked the staff glad of work
after months at the food bank.
How to tip when cash is untouchable?

•

11 years later 2/7 Lower Nine schools reopened.
Next door in St. Bernard Parish
all schools back in two years.
Walk the streets in both
zones look at the people
look at their colours.

•

Some of the rebuilt projects look like Disney World.

I picked a place of loss.
Picked the route with the most Goldilocks layover
the best food options the best window view
to point a camera at. Clicked
"purchase."

Went farther and imagined
looking in from out there and saw me
here at my desk but I was neither
here nor there. I was not
anywhere. A body sat here

that was mine. Words on the screen
emerged. Time goes differently
          in there. *Longer than you think.*

Years after on the Ucluelet sand a table
from across the sea. A door,
some planks. On Haida Gwaii, a motorcycle.
In Oregon, a boat with fish.
Cans that can't be
recycled here, contents
guzzled before the quake, the wave.

Morning humid the noise of late
summer waft of riversmell. You long
from away and nowhere
in that place longs back.

TASHME (BC, Here, 2017)

Here is an original door.
The fox barn with its octagon window.
The large barn was once apartments.
This plant, fuki, for which residents
ordered packs of seeds from Japan or asked
their former neighbours to send
from plants still growing, has taken
over. These crabapple trees
were here then. Some
who took the tour remembered
picking the fruit. The highway
wasn't here. The Sumallo's course
was altered in the early '80s. All this
was shacks. The Stop of Interest
designation finally approved. The maps
will change. This took a long time. The younger girl
thought I wasn't coming back. She took
her sister's and her grandpa's hands and led them
off to look for me down the old road. Crying
like it was all over forever, I learned later.
When we got back to the museum
they weren't there nor at the playground
with the real teeter-totter. Old but not
here then. Kids in wedding party clothes
up and down. Far in the distance
three figures by the horse stables. Brush-
strokes. The small ones
running toward me.

—I saw a guy hang onto a column with his camera
trying to film. Then I hear the windows shatter. Bang
bang bang bang. —It looked like somebody had taken the plug
out of the sea. —It looked quite lovely… We were
spellbound. —I filmed the scene again
and again. I said to myself, hey what a perfect
wave. —We should warn the tourists. What if
that wave hits the beach. —You carry on filming.
—And then in that moment I knew how big the wave was.

If a wrapped square stone is sitting on the stairs
or on the path to the tea room, don't go that way.

When she goes
there will be nowhere to.
A favourite place a box of ash
blown in my face by the ocean.
We'll be the only evidence
there was such a room
that held us that rocked that stretched
as big as we needed with water.

Convenience store.
Traffic stop.
Their rooms there without them.

The tickets scanned my face scanned the printout of my face scanned
and set on a pile. *—Just going to meet my brother from Vancouver
and enjoy the city for a bit.* Research interests: Ruin porn.
Is that poorism? The box I checked said "personal."

LOWER NINE (New Orleans, Here, 2016)

On a bike bumping over old roads bad roads
leaning weeds narrowing Deslonde
and potholes and a few houses a few people
and hot and real and grit and not alone.

•

Lots to clear decks to build
houses still to gut. Lots of weeds lots of mattresses
and bags of trash and trash.

Less haunting
than on Street View.

People live here.

•

Doveweed. Virginia buttonweed.

Gripeweed chamber bitter or mimosa weed.

Oxalis. Dollarweed.

•

The German landscape architecture editor
shares my hand sanitizer.
We're the two who stop to photograph.
No gluten for her three bags of chips no
meat for me takeout shrimp fried rice
from the Vietnamese family
at Cajun Joe's nowhere to recycle
not the greatest education says the guide
who lived it our leftovers in Styrofoam
for the volunteers in the trailer
that's the House of Dance and Feathers
the museum of Mardi Gras Indians of Social
Aid & Pleasure Clubs of Skull & Bone Gangs.
The man whose house was moved
how many blocks spends his days here
amidst the costumes all year stitching.

Eau de printemps 2020.

Resilience as feathers.
How long the Styrofoam the feathers.

•

In the sliver by the river
the flood was lowest. The levee
higher than the houses the blue
tarps still on Holy Cross High School
the old locks still on the lockers.
Market? Condos?

•

First four years just gutting.
If it's solid, heritage, keep the shell,
make a new inside.
No dozers or plastic orange fences.

Let the memories begin.

•

The Executive Director
of the non-profit
rolls down the window
for my camera. Okays the recorder.
Shows me the ADA compliant curbs
on blocks where no one lives.
The man with half his teeth
asks what I'm writing down. The sound files
end up overlayered our voices atop
our voices when I get home I can't
tell what she's saying. My notes
scribbles. On the bike if I stop
the rest go on ahead.

In the film, citizens demolish where they lived
so the Yangtze can flow over.

This is how to generate power.

Inside a chrysalis is snot, a mush no one
can watch. Comes out new, remembers
what the old self knew.

Both dead, my Superman, my Lois.
He fell from a horse and lived and died.
Her mind did her in. At first the news said
    Peacefully. A while later, Suicide. *A big relief,*
    her daughter said, *that the truth is out there.*

The clenching fist the sign meaning milk,
hunger, comfort,
boredom, I want I want love me I don't
know what I want.

To select different
options, click here.

At a shelter someone waits for his brother.
Until there's evidence he won't come
he might. How long until
no proof is proof.

Our balls of string
shine like no balls of string
ever did our balls of rubber
bands. Look on Pinterest
look out Instagram.

Fuki, a.k.a. *Petasites japonicus.*
Butterbur, great butterbur, giant butterbur,
sweet-coltsfoot. Pre-treat with ash
or baking soda and soak in water to remove
astringency, 灰汁抜き,
bitterness removal.

Why the woman who set herself on fire in the line
people come each day to wait in when there are families still in Houston.
Why the Congolese boy scaling the razor wire fence to what
freedom. The man who fled Honduras with his son
made it to Texas was sent back kidnapped in Mexico eventually
returned to Honduras. When there are millions.
Why not this one thing enough this one wrong.
She wiped his organs from his mouth with her hand.

The man who fled talked to
This American Life.
Saved enough to fly to Spain.
Then COVID hit.
As of broadcast time had not
gone outside.

We arrived at the castle on the last day.
The big-eared mice were celebrating at high pitch.
Snow that was bubbles drifted toward us, Elsa's cape
blown suddenly back though it was hot, windless.
We were not in America.
There was no wall.
We had paid to come.
We had felt joy.
Of course she sang "Let It Go."
The women and men from Puerto Rico and Haiti,
the university student from Osceola,
names and places on their badges,
they were smiling.
We didn't want to go home.
As the daily parade festooned Main Street
the woman who worked in the Confectionery
sang like she meant it.
We pretended it was for us.

LOWER NINE (New Orleans, Still Here, 2016)

Top architects built
top drawer blue chip homes
no gutters but solar panels
the electricity bill's so cheap!
If you can get a mortgage.

•

Roughly 36.7% of pre-Katrina pop.
Maybe 10 or 15% the same people.

•

Ghosts need sheets so we see them
O my lord. Everywhere my lord.

•

When she's lived here a decade rebuilding
when she's bought a house
in the sliver by the river
when the older guy she's known for years
        says *Hello darlin' you slummin' again*
when he's Black when she's White
when he's American when she was Canadian when
we're in her car getting the tour when
he's joking when they laugh when
I'm silent.

•

Many still living my lord.

•

At each public meeting
there's prayer. At least three meetings
each week. Assuming one prayer
per meeting that's 156 per year
2 028 since she started.
Eighty-eight homes rebuilt
and counting.
23.05 prayers a home.

Those are just the ones she hears.

•

Resilience is futile
says a t-shirt she's not wearing.

Each day will be a day farther from the day
we learned he was dead but he will never be less dead.
Will he be more dead or was he most dead when it was first said
he was. And the girls asked what and the world blurred
the path by the creek of stones the bridge we didn't cross.

House of Julia Felix.
House of Loreius Tiburtinus.

House of Menander.
House of Sallust.

House of the Tragic Poet.
Temple of Isis (Pompeii)

6441 Louis XIV Street.
House of the handcuffs.

Will paradise tear death?
You will be with me. Perfection
degenerate. Crush foretelling.
Who will reside blameless.

Machines draw the New Safe Confinement
over the ills, over and over
as many times as you want
till the eyes are sealed.

—The road to my house did not exist anymore.

Two bodies still somewhere under
the Hope Slide, a marker
there for decades. Six minutes
up the road where Tashme was
a sign for the first time.

He waited a year to listen to his favourite
album so it would be better. He waited months
to end his life so it would mean something.

Next time we will build it right.

Get on the bus without looking back.

We won't issue the order we will see the water coming we will climb the hill.

AT THE END (The World)

They raised this son up. Proud he was
to have left them.

At the end on the phone from his house
on the ledge of granite
he said he wondered
what the adventure would be.

•

She drank a slush of 7-Up.
Her pulse slowed until undetectable;
she persisted. She who crosswords who haiku who choir
who daughter who granddaughter who files of vacation brochures.
She who *soupe + dessert, pas de plat principal.*
At the service she agreed to
for them, bookmarks with her face.

•

At the end in a bed in a hospital she burped and farted and forgot.

•

She wanted a glass of water.

•

Fifteen years after lots of songbirds
lots full of weeds.

•

Beyond the end of everything is nothing,
which is not the same as space.

The room reels out, a gust of birds.

On the shortest day there is light
on the dry grasses in the meadow.
We come out of the forest.

Elysian Fields where we've dreamt of going
since the ancients. Desire where every year
there's a Stella-calling contest, where
we turn the corner on our bikes
signalling that old way with our arms.

The window shut the blinds opening
the blue door across the street.

They have gone in the short dark woman
the tall pale man they are home. Now it's dark.

COVID brought her parents from Toronto
(from Vietnam originally from China) to live there.
Each morning afternoon sometimes early
evening they lurch out in masks
and then come back.
At night, they sing and watch Chinese TV.

Olives set out for guests
still here millennia after. Shrivelled
to stones behind glass
in a city of marvel.

The Chernobyl Exclusion Zone
has its magic in every season.

Disney says *Help us protect the magic.*
Please limit handling of the product.

She got up early for me to braid her hair
but still there was no time. She left
in -30 her face behind the ice
window of the bus her sister's face
beside her. They couldn't see me either.
In the morning's exhaust I turned back to the house.

That wrecked bed blackened if you blew on it
the embers would glow as stones
lit from within and you could rest.

The little yellows that are greens.
The little flowers that are leaves.

Can you spare just five minutes to help us create a better world?

Too many windows
left open.

RAIN (Rain)

Rain on the lake willows.

Rain on the shore willows.

Rain on the swallow house.

Rain on the swallow.

Rain on the ash treated with a pesticide.

Rain on the lawn treated with an herbicide.

Rain on the mallards.

Rain on the lakeshore mansions and the vacant apartments.

Rain on the ice cream stand.

Rain on the flavours.

Rain on the planters of begonias and bougainvilleas.

Rain on the crying girl.

Rain on the library.

Rain on the naptime the little tent the dolls left out.

Rain on the playhouse the swings the twisty slide.

Rain on the levee.

Rain on the river.

Rain on the fresh-washed car.

Rain elsewhere.

Rain on the goldenrod.

Rain on the uppermost branches.

Rain on the lowermost roots.

Rain in runnels down the trunk.

Rain on the clicks of the red-winged blackbirds.

Rain on the reactor.

Rain on the gravel.

Rain where the fireworks will burst.

Rain on the dryer huff.

Rain on the doormat the umbrella left out.

Rain on the e-mail.

Rain on the name.

Rain on my friend in Montara California.

Rain on her drive to make enough to live in Montara California.

Rain on her husband not yet dead.

Rain on Nicholas and William.

Rain on Aidan.

Rain on Gabrielle, Félix, and Myriam.

Rain on Naomi and Isabel and long-gone never gone Josephine.

Rain on Isabel and Chloe.

Rain on Hannah the palindrome.

Rain on rain on rain.

Rain on Patrick and André.

Rain on David, Cindy, Barbara, Tim, and Danny.

Rain on Curran.

Rain on Chris and Tobias.

Rain on Sara and Peter.

Rain on Stephanie and Kevin.

Rain on Madeleine and Éloïse.

Rain on the eyelids.

Rain on the tongue.

Rain on the drought.

Rain on the parched crops.

Rain on the parched soil.

Rain over the parched soul.

Rain in runnels past the fields.

Rain that the reservoirs.

Rain that California.

Rain that Vancouver.

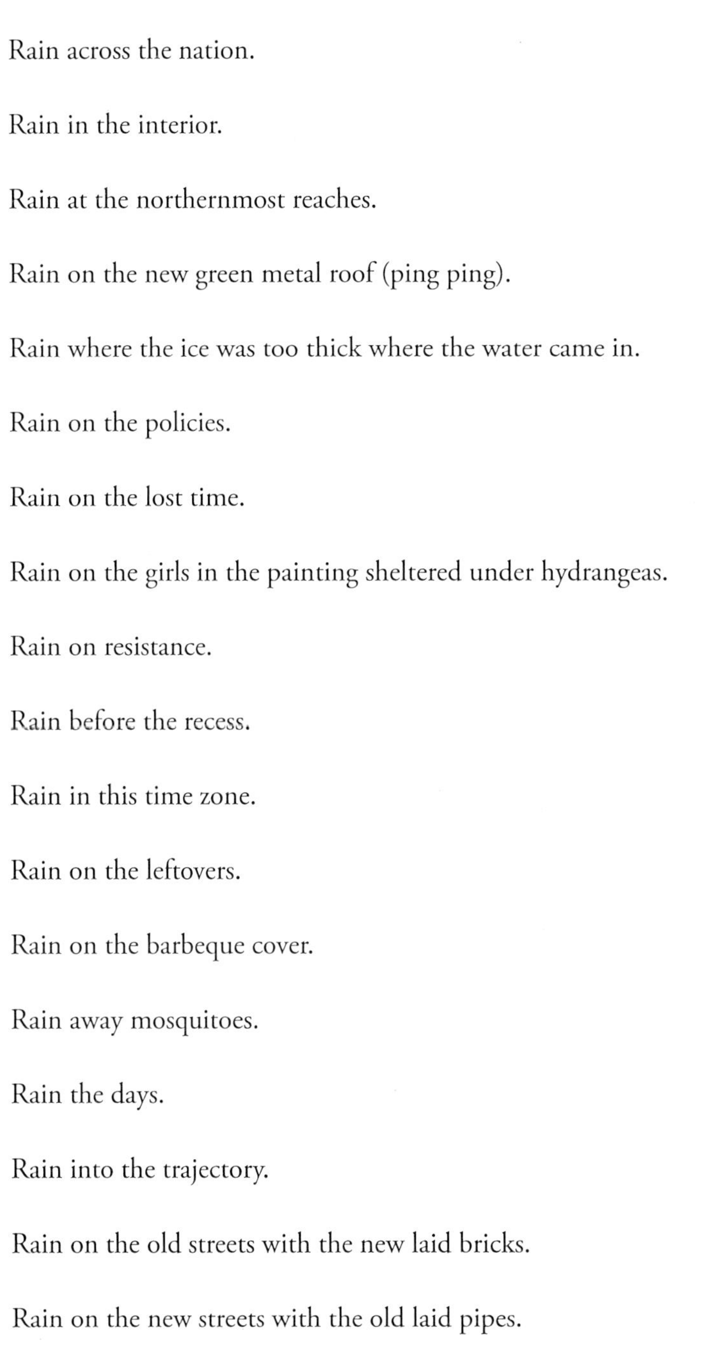

Rain across the nation.

Rain in the interior.

Rain at the northernmost reaches.

Rain on the new green metal roof (ping ping).

Rain where the ice was too thick where the water came in.

Rain on the policies.

Rain on the lost time.

Rain on the girls in the painting sheltered under hydrangeas.

Rain on resistance.

Rain before the recess.

Rain in this time zone.

Rain on the leftovers.

Rain on the barbeque cover.

Rain away mosquitoes.

Rain the days.

Rain into the trajectory.

Rain on the old streets with the new laid bricks.

Rain on the new streets with the old laid pipes.

Rain on the land.

Rain on the landfill.

Rain on the community.

Rain on resilience.

Rain on the house my father grew up in.

Rain on the house my mother grew up in.

Rain on the walnut tree rain on the gooseberries.

Rain on the pond and all the gone and golden fishes.

Rain on the bathroom my brother got locked in.

Rain on the basement room my uncle slept in.

Rain on the character home rain on the laneway house.

Rain on the stairs and rain on the railing.

Rain on the dandelions.

Rain on the demolitions.

Rain on the celebrities.

Rain where the canaries were rain where the stray cats.

Rain on the chicken in its wire and the chicken who went missing.

Rain on the chicken bought on Kijiji who died in a day and went to the landfill.

Rain on the peacocks of the privileged.

Rain on acceptance.

Rain on Bulgaria.

Rain on Rhodesia.

Rain on the former places.

Rain at the end of the nineteenth century.

Rain on Lordship Lane.

Rain where they came from.

Rain on the Caribbean.

Rain where we came from.

Rain on Landcroft Road.

Rain where my grandmother left.

Rain where my grandmother arrived.

Rain on the people there for millennia.

Rain on the belongings.

Rain where I stood.

Rain on the photograph.

Rain on the Zoom sessions.

Rain on the fires.

Rain of the last century.

Rain on the community.

Rain on the newfound apartment.

Rain on the unanticipated sadness.

Rain on Lost River.

Rain on the future.

Rain on the last places rain on the first places.

Rain on the unsigned places.

Rain on Diana.

Rain on Anya.

Rain on Ernie.

Rain on Edna.

Rain on Arn.

Rain on Elise.

Rain on Laura.

Rain on Danny.

Rain on Jay.

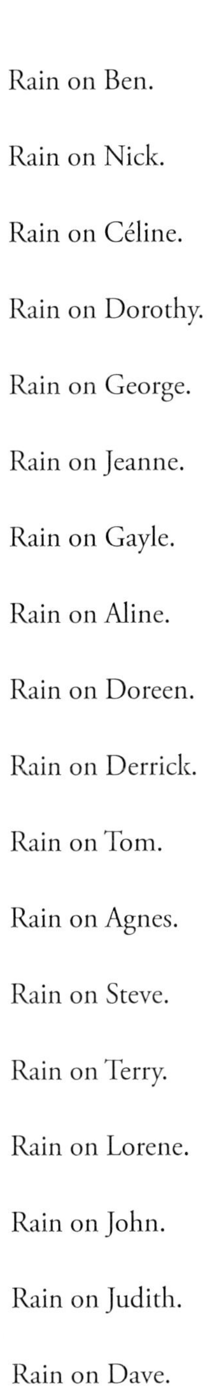

Rain on Ben.

Rain on Nick.

Rain on Céline.

Rain on Dorothy.

Rain on George.

Rain on Jeanne.

Rain on Gayle.

Rain on Aline.

Rain on Doreen.

Rain on Derrick.

Rain on Tom.

Rain on Agnes.

Rain on Steve.

Rain on Terry.

Rain on Lorene.

Rain on John.

Rain on Judith.

Rain on Dave.

Rain on the voyage.

Rain on the waves.

Rain on the names.

Rain on the graves.

Rain on the Victorian era.

Rain on the Victrola.

Rain on the grand piano.

Rain on clematis.

Rain on the trellis.

Rain on the darkness.

Rain into the darkness.

Rain on the dinosaurs.

Rain on the trailers.

Rain on the trains.

Rain on the awning of the famous café.

Rain on the place people used to dance.

Rain on the continent.

Rain in the well.

NOTES ON THE TEXT

The Japanese phrases translate as follows: こどものために *Kodomo no tame ni* – "For the sake of the children" (p. 20), しかたがない *Shikata ga nai* – "It can't be helped" (p. 20, 44, and 60), 孤独死 *Kodoku-shi* – "Lonely death" (p. 81), and 灰汁抜き *aku nuki* – "bitterness removal" (p. 118).

Italicized material on pages 25 ("*Lectures should be pre-recorded*"), 39 ("*He does not wear the coat*"), 50 ("*Displacement in the wake of devastating*"), and 109 ("*Love is long-suffering")* has been condensed from the original, with typographical indicators of ellipses dropped.

ACKNOWLEDGEMENTS

I am indebted to many citizens, writers, researchers, and artists whose words, images, and work has informed mine. A complete, detailed list of citations may be found here:

In the order in which their words or work appear, thank you to: Robert Polidori (and Robert Ayers, Beatrice Zamponi, Payal Uttam, Rachel Duffell, and Michèle Gelber Klein, who reported Polidori's words), Philip Gourevitch, Jay Farrar and Son Volt, Elizabeth Kolbert, John Updike, Peirce Lewis, John Brack (and Becky Little, who reported Brack's words), David Lynch (and Zack Sharf, who reported Lynch's words), Will Robins, Lyudmilla Ignatenko, Aleksandr Kudryagin, and many others who survived the Chernobyl disaster (and Svetlana Alexievich, who presented their words, and Keith Gessen, who translated them), Linda Villarosa, Sergey Krasilnikov (and Kim Hjelmgaard, who reported Krasilnikov's story), Herbert Freeman Jr. and many others who survived Hurricane Katrina and the levee breaches (and Spike Lee, who presented their words), Joy Kogawa, Genevieve Hansen, Charles McMillian, Alyssa (surname undisclosed), Donald Williams, Linda Ohama (and her family, featured in the documentary film *Obachan's Garden*), Kim Peatfield, Allison Plyer, Concordia University, Kate Brown, Aleksandr Kudryagin, British Columbia Security Commission Report, Michael Maltese, Amnesty

International, Mike Theiss and Jim Reid, Caroline Bologna, Cindy Sherwin and Adam Kovac, Geoff Dyer, Madeleine Leroux, Ann Gomer Sunahara, Howard Shimokura (and Jennifer Moreau, who reported Shimokura's words), Wallace Stevens, the Takahashi Family, Tak Negoro, Masako Fukawa, Alice Reid, Louann Mims (and the team at *This American Life*, who reported Mims' story and those of many others), Lori Nix, Paulette Gagnon, Michael Stipe and R.E.M., Emily Zemler, Michael Koren, Percy Bysshe Shelley, Anonymous, Diana Brebner, Joanne Watts, Woody Allen, Leanne Sarco, Dr. Homa Hoodfar (and Ashifa Kassam, who reported Hoodfar's story), Dani Anguiano, the Nikkei National Museum & Cultural Centre, Jane Werner Watson, Ralph Blumenthal, Austin E. Anson, George Henry Powell ("George Asal"), Donald Weber, Naomi Hiratsuka (and Julian Ryall, who reported Hiratsuka's story), Wendell Pierce, Dennis Normile, Bianca Nogrady, Laura Paul, Canada Life, Rebecca Onion, Philip Kahn (and Katharine Q. Seelye, who reported Kahn's story), Louisiana State Museum, Dani McClain, Haing Ngor (and Deirdre Donohue, who reported Ngor's words), Ian McCulloch and Echo and the Bunnymen, Andrei Tarkovsky, Rebecca Solnit, David Guttenfelder, Miyu Kojima, City of Pointe-Claire, Andy Warhol, Emily St. John Mandel, Sandon Museum, William Bryant Logan, Éloïse Leroux, Emma Donoghue, Theodor Seuss Geisel (Dr. Seuss), Raphael Dallaporta, David Maisel, Heather Smith, Nicholas Shapiro, Sunshine Valley RV Resort & Cabins, The Chernobyl Gallery, Sergei Zabolotnyy, Lydia Haywood Munn, Leonard Cohen, Stephen King, Andrew Stones, Fredrik Bornesand, Mark Heather, Stefan Kühn, and other unidentified survivors of the 26 December 2004 tsunami (and Janice Sutherland, who presented their stories), Montreal Botanical Garden, Dan Gill, Ronald W. Lewis, Disney World, Jia Zhangke, Maggie McGuane (and Matt Volz, who reported McGuane's words), Laura Paul, Bill Waiters, and lowernine.org; Bedu Saini, Brooks Barnes, Hannah Lownsbrough, and, of course, Wikipedia.

What began in 2009 as an interrogation of my unsettling fascination with Robert Polidori's photographs of post-Katrina New Orleans became an education that has lasted for 16 years and does not end here. I am grateful to those who have supported this project, reading drafts, asking questions, and posing challenges.

For thoughtful reading and for his perspective that begins in slavery and is rooted in the Lower Ninth Ward, thank you to John Frasier Smith ("Smitty"). Howard Shimokura, Tak Negoro, Leanne Sarco, Sara Graefe, Maureen Medved, Merise Brebner, and Michael Shaw granted permission to share their experiences, a generosity for which I will always be grateful. Deep and enduring thanks to Barbara Nickel and Christopher Patton for their insights into early and later drafts – for helping me to stem and honour the flood. Without them, this book would not exist in this form. Without their unwavering faith and friendship, I might have turned away from these challenges. John Wall Barger read with discernment and enthusiasm and has cheered me on for years; thank you. Thanks to Sara Graefe for writing with me through the final stages and then the final final stages. Thank you to Laura Paul, Executive Director of lowernine.org for taking time to show me the Lower Nine and for sustained support and readings since. Thank you to Lisa Uyeda, Collections Manager and Daien Ide, Research Archivist at the Nikkei National Museum & Cultural Centre, for finding the files and helping me secure permissions, and to Ryan Ellan, founder of the Tashme Museum, for taking (and talking) me around the site. Robert Polidori found me several years into this project his photographs initiated; his encouragement propelled me, as the complexity of his work sustained me. I'm grateful for his generosity in granting permission to reproduce his photograph on the cover without fees. I'm also grateful to Concordia University, which has offered support through community, sabbaticals, and a professional development allowance. Thank you to the students with whom I've had the pleasure, honour, and challenge of working; you remind me what matters. Thank you to my teachers, from whom I am still learning. Thank you to my families – the one I was born into and the one I've been given – for love, patience, support, and engagement.

I have tried to track down all of those whose stories – first shared with journalists and documentary filmmakers – I've drawn from here. While my intention is to honour their voices, I didn't want to assume that, having put their stories into the public sphere, they'd support their inclusion here. I cut many passages whose speakers/authors I could not locate or who could not give permission. A few seemed essential enough to keep, and I hope they will understand why. If your experience is here and I haven't found you yet, please contact me.

An excerpt from the "Long Exposure" strand was a finalist for the CBC Poetry Prize in 2012; an excerpt from "Shelter Object" was a finalist in 2019, after having been (in an earlier form) longlisted in 2017. Other excerpts have appeared in *The Angle*, *The Antigonish Review*, *Contemporary Verse 2*, *Eighteen Bridges*, *Grain*, *The Fiddlehead*, *Literary Review of Canada*, *Numero Cinq*, *Ottawater*, *Painted Bride Quarterly* (U.S.), *Cordite Poetry Review* (Australia), and on the CBC website, as well as in *The Best of Canadian Poetry in English 2022*, the chapbook *Ghosts* (above/ground press, 2017) and as an above/ground press broadside. Thank you to the editors of these publications.

Author proceeds from the sale of this book will be donated equally to lowernine.org (New Orleans, LA) and the Nikkei National Museum & Cultural Centre (Burnaby, BC).

PHOTO CREDIT: PATRICK LEROUX

Stephanie Bolster has published four previous books, the first of which, *White Stone: The Alice Poems*, won the Governor General's Award and the Gerald Lampert Award. She edited *The Best Canadian Poetry 2008* and *The Ishtar Gate: Last and Selected Poems* by Diana Brebner, and co-edited *Penned: Zoo Poems*. Born in Vancouver, she lives in Pointe-Claire, Quebec, on the traditional territories of the Kanien'kehá:ka people, and teaches in the creative writing program at Concordia University.